SELF HARM
THE PATH TO
RECOVERY

**Dr Kate Middleton
and Sara Garvie**

LION

A Lion Book
an imprint of
Lion Hudson plc
Wilkinson House, Jordan Hill Road,
Oxford OX2 8DR, England
www.lionhudson.com
ISBN 978 0 7459 5319 9 (print)
ISBN 978 0 7459 5810 1 (epub)
ISBN 978 0 7459 5809 5 (Kindle)
ISBN 978 0 7459 5811 8 (pdf)

First edition 2008
10 9 8 7 6 5 4 3 2 1 0

A catalogue record for this book is available
from the British Library

Typeset in 10/13 Iowan OldStyle

Printed and bound in Great Britain by
Marston Book Services Ltd, Oxfordshire

Contents

Introduction

People call self harm all kinds of things – a phenomenon, a 'mental health problem' – I have even heard it referred to as a 'maladaptive tool for emotional regulation'. But what I know most of all is that self harm is a real thing that affects real people.

Self harm can be very frightening, and not just for people on the outside. Often the people who are most scared are those who are doing it. One thing that working with people who are struggling with all kinds of emotional and psychological problems has taught me, however, is that 'normal' people can be driven to do things that feel very extreme when they are under the pressure of extraordinary emotions. They haven't gone 'crazy', and they are usually no less 'normal' than any of the rest of us.

My little girl has a book about a strange creature hiding behind a curtain. It makes unusual noises and terrifies the characters as they wonder what is hiding there. It's a lot less scary when they find out it's a dog! You see, almost anything can be frightening if you don't know what it is. And that's often a big part of the problem with self harm. Self harm can be scary, dangerous and out of control, but that doesn't mean that it can't be explained and understood. This book is about trying to help people understand it better, and we hope that helps it become a lot less frightening.

In this book, in between the chapters talking about the theory and practical reality of self harm, you will find stories from real people talking about their experiences of self harm. I can't thank enough the people who shared their stories with us. I hope that these will help you to understand the truth of what self harm is. Remember that everyone is different – and every sufferer's story of their self harm is different. The personal accounts have not been included to show you what self harm is always like – and they are in themselves very different. They are there to give you an idea of the kinds of experiences people have, and to show the very varied paths people can travel as part of their road to recovery.

One thing worth mentioning if you are someone who currently self harms, or who used to, is that we are aware that you may find talking about certain aspects of harming 'triggering' – that is, that reading or thinking about them might make you want to harm. Obviously, in a book about self harm we can't avoid these topics and we've done everything we can to prevent triggering. Do be sensible, however. If you know you are vulnerable, then this might not be the book to read when you are on your own or at a low moment. But we hope that overall it will bring you hope.

About the book...
This book has three sections. Part 1 looks at what self harm is and who it affects, along with trying to answer some of the questions around why it is so addictive. Part 2 then looks in a bit more detail at some of the emotional, psychological and practical issues behind self harm and offers advice for how to start working on recovery. Part 3 is written for those caring for sufferers, be that as parents or in a professional role. At the end of the book there is some extra information on dealing with scars, along with some links and guidance about where to look for more help.

Because of the nature of the book, some sections are written as though we are speaking just to sufferers, carers or professionals. That doesn't mean that those chapters are not of use if that isn't you – so do read them and take what is discussed on board. Although they may be aimed at one group of people in particular, it is likely that wherever you are coming from you will find them interesting – and the more you understand about self harm, the better a position you will be in.

This book is written from real-life experiences that Sara

and I have had of working with sufferers. I personally have been privileged to work with some fantastic people who have bravely started out on a journey of recovery, and trusted me to show them the way. This book is dedicated to them, and to anyone out there who is facing that struggle now. You are worth so much more than you realize. Please don't give up, and know that recovery and freedom *is possible*. We pray that this book helps you to start to find some light pricking through the darkness you are living with.

Kate Middleton

Part 1

What is self harm and how does it develop?

1 What is self harm?

'It just took me totally by surprise. I mean, I knew she was having problems but I didn't know that it had got so... out of control. I just didn't know what to do or how to react, or what she was expecting me to do... I mean, it was just never heard of when I was younger. Now I hear that loads of people are doing it and I just don't understand why – I mean, how can it possibly be helpful to hurt yourself? How can that possibly make you feel better, and why on earth do people get drawn to it?'
JAN, MUM OF A SIXTEEN-YEAR-OLD WHO HAS BEEN SELF HARMING FOR THREE YEARS

'I don't really know why I started it. I know it's what people always want to ask me, but I just don't really know. There was such a lot going on, and some days I felt like my head would just explode. Everyone else seemed to be yelling a lot and crying, but I don't do those things. I guess one day I just needed some way to get it out somehow and that's when it all started.'
HELENA, TWENTY-ONE, WHO HAS BEEN SELF HARMING NOW FOR SIX YEARS

I wonder what has brought you to pick up this book today? Some of you will be reading it because you self harm. Some will be trying to find out more about what someone else is doing. Or perhaps you are just trying to find out more about a problem that used to be very unusual or even unheard of – and now affects so many people in the UK.

Self harm is something that most people find difficult to understand – a destructive impulse that doesn't seem to make sense. Both sufferers and those who care for them sometimes find it hard not to feel critical towards those who self harm, and struggle with feelings of disgust about the wounds and the mess self harm creates. The reality, however, is that for millions of people in the UK right now self harm is something that they do regularly to help them cope with feelings that are out of control. In fact, self harm has increased dramatically in frequency in the UK over the last ten years. What used to be unusual and seen only in a small proportion of mental health patients now occurs in most schools, universities and clinics across the country. To understand why this is happening, we need to understand what self harm is, and how something that seems so destructive can become very addictive.

Let's take the chance right now to explain clearly what we mean by the term 'self harm'. Self harm is generally defined as *acting to deliberately injure yourself physically*. The exact form of harm varies, and ranges from minor, occasional acts to more serious and regular harm that can require hospital treatment. Some forms of self harm are invisible or do not leave a wound. These can include acts of hitting or punching or taking substances that cause pain or discomfort. Other forms create a visible wound, such as cutting or burning the skin. This kind of self harm is statistically the most common, with around two out of three sufferers saying that they use cutting as their main method. Meanwhile, some other sufferers may show more unusual kinds of self harm, such as deliberately breaking bones or pulling out hairs.[1] Some people always harm in the same way; others use different methods according to what is available at the time. Some sufferers may harm specific parts of their body, whilst others may use anywhere that would be hidden by clothing.

---

1 Pulling out hairs forms a separate diagnostic category for clinicians and is called trichotillomania.

One very important thing to be clear about when we use the term 'self harm' is the difference between self harm and acts that are part of an attempt to end life. Some research studies and medical papers use the term 'deliberate self harm' to include actions of attempted suicide, and it can be difficult to distinguish the two, particularly if very similar actions are involved – such as cutting wrists or taking overdoses. However, we do not include those things in our discussion because we – and the people we work with and support – find the distinction clear. The easiest way to understand the difference is to look at what that person intended to happen as a result of their actions. The self harm we are describing is not intended to end life. Instead it forms part of a coping strategy that the sufferer develops in order to help them to deal with emotions and feelings that are overwhelming. Self harm is an attempt to stop the barrage of emotion, depression and anxiety, to escape the accusatory thoughts that plague sufferers and to find a moment of peace and freedom.

Having said that, it is very important to be aware that self harm is often very closely linked to suicidal thoughts and attempts. Statistically those who self harm are many times more likely to attempt suicide than those who do not. Even those who are not suicidal may risk their life unintentionally if their harming becomes very serious. Most teenagers say they harm in an attempt to express distress and escape difficult situations. But every year some lose their lives, even though this was not their aim. It is important to be aware that the feelings that trigger self harm are very powerful. These are not people who are just feeling 'a bit down'. Instead, powerful emotions – combined with repeated episodes of anxiety and depression – mean that many sufferers become increasingly desperate, and struggle to hold on to any hope of recovery or change. With that hopelessness can easily come thoughts of suicide. The dividing line between self harm and suicide can get increasingly thin, particularly for individuals who have suffered for a long time.

All this means that our definition of self harm needs to be expanded. In this book, therefore, when we use the term 'self harm' we mean *acting to deliberately injure yourself physically in an attempt to cope with, express or reduce intense or overwhelming emotions*. This is a slightly different definition from that used in, for example, the NICE (National Institute of Clinical Excellence) guidelines for self harm,[2] and we hope that our reasons for making this distinction are clear. In common with NICE, however, we prefer the term 'self harm' to 'deliberate self harm'. This is because, as we will discuss later in the book, some people harm when not fully in control of their actions, so we feel the word 'deliberate' is not always accurate. This book aims to discuss, explain and demystify self harm and to offer practical advice to help people cope with this issue as well as start to work towards recovery.

Now that we are clear what we mean by self harm, the next question usually asked is why people do it. This question, together with what makes self harm such an addictive behaviour, will be considered in more depth in Chapters 3 and 4, but in understanding what self harm *is* it's important to be aware of the ways in which its exact nature can vary from sufferer to sufferer. Self harm is about doing something to yourself that has a negative physical outcome. It is a powerful communication of how intense emotional pain has become. Some people see self harm as a form of punishment, whilst for others there is something else in the act that helps them deal with how they are feeling – perhaps the visible wound, the releasing of blood or the experience of physical pain. For others self harm occurs impulsively

---

2 They use the definition 'self-poisoning or self-injury, irrespective of the apparent purpose of the act'.

and almost instinctively as a response to an emotion such as anger or frustration. This emotion is often directed inwardly, and sufferers become increasingly frustrated and angry with themselves, culminating in the harming. Sometimes self harm can become part of a deliberate and planned response to emotional pain. Sufferers report starting to feel overwhelmed by a desire to harm as their emotions build and become increasingly out of control. Self harm may then follow a strict routine.

So far we have talked about the kinds of self harm that are usually included in definitions and discussions on this topic. However, some people have argued that other behaviours which, although widely practised, also have possible or inevitable negative physical outcomes, should be included as types of self harm – such as alcohol abuse, smoking, unsafe sex and even eating disorders like anorexia and bulimia. Most people would not include these things when they talk about self harm, but it is certainly true that some people deliberately engage in such risky or unhealthy behaviours whilst in the negative emotional spirals that can be part of self harm. Therefore, sometimes it is appropriate to include such actions when considering the ways a person self harms. Eating disorders form a special case, with so many sufferers also self harming that the two are often very strongly linked. Some people with eating disorders specifically consider some of the things they do to be kinds of self harm. They might talk about purging to 'punish' themselves, or see pain experienced as something they 'deserve'. So in this way behaviours that are part of another disorder can overlap with what we might consider to be self harm. Ultimately, almost any behaviour or addiction that has a negative physical outcome could potentially be part of a wider continuum of self harm.

Another hotly debated area of 'self harm' is the question of body piercing and tattooing. Most professionals agree that such things, done apparently as an expression of style and as a statement of some kind, can in fact sometimes be a form of self harm. However, many people who have numerous body piercings or tattoos would challenge this opinion. Our experience is that some self harmers have used the promised reward of a new piercing to try to stop harming, and that others use piercings and tattoos as a form of self harm. This doesn't mean everyone who has their ears pierced is self harming, and it is usually seen in those who have multiple piercings or tattoos done in a short space of time. So again, it is important to be aware of the possibility that some people might be vulnerable to using this behaviour as a form of self harm.

All this demonstrates clearly that there are many different ways in which people self harm – and that one person's pattern of self harm may well be different from another person's. If there's one thing that most sufferers have in common, however, it is that self harm is usually more than a one-off occurrence. In fact, if you look at people who have self harmed once, you'll see that well over half will go on to start doing it regularly. Self harm is part of an attempt to find a way of coping with extreme and painful emotions. Self-harm acts are often triggered by difficult emotions, and it is common to see a pattern of people harming in an attempt to bring an end to a horrible emotional experience. However, self harm is a temporary solution. Whatever the more complex reason behind why people do it, the relief is only short term. The problems and difficult feelings and emotions that triggered it are usually unresolved, and until that person gets help or finds that their situation changes, they will generally continue to struggle. Self harm is not an effective way of coping with emotions in the long term. In fact, because of the feelings it triggers, together with issues like isolation and guilt, self harm can, in the long run, make things much worse.

Real-life experiences...
Introducing some people with experience of self harm

Throughout this book we are going to introduce you to four people – Nina, Jim, Rachael and Libby – who are happy to share their experiences of working through self harm with you. We'll look at their stories four times in total throughout the book and share their journeys with them. These are real stories; they are not case studies or made-up examples. They offer some insight into what self harm is really like and give you a snapshot of these people's experiences of recovery. Remember, everyone is different and these are just four of the millions of people in the UK who have been through self harm. Let's start by hearing them talk about when their self harm began.

NINA
'I still remember the first time I hurt myself really clearly. It was a spring evening and about nine months after I'd moved out of home into my own place. Life just felt as if it was getting on top of me. I was crying and crying and I couldn't stop. I felt hopeless, useless and so, so alone. I knelt on the floor, picked up my hairbrush and hit my leg with it in sheer frustration. I was almost shocked I'd hit myself; shocked enough to stop me crying for a bit, which was kind of a relief. But I also still hurt so much – inside, in a way I couldn't really quite describe. So I hit my arm. As hard as I could, and again and again. The more I hit it the more it hurt. But it almost felt better to make the pain into something real. I kept hitting, lots of little hits by now making my arm redder and redder. Somehow it was quite satisfying. Afterwards I felt awful about it. How could I have done that? Wasn't that something weird people did? Lots of things were wrong, but I'd been really upset lots of times before and I wasn't

quite sure why this time it was worse than usual. None of it quite made sense. But I could see the visible evidence of the pain that I still had no words to describe and somehow it made me feel a bit better.

'On the outside there weren't really a lot of reasons for feeling so bad inside. I grew up in a really "normal" environment, with a family who I know love me. There was nothing you'd outwardly pinpoint as leading me to develop anorexia, though I did, at the start of my second year at university. At the time I started to harm I was doing reasonably well in recovering from anorexia physically but still ignoring most of the underlying stuff. Inside I was a mess, and hardly anyone knew that I was crying on the way to work, at lunchtime, on the way home and most evenings for nearly nine months. Self harm became a way of dealing with things. I didn't hit myself again for another year, but I'd pick at my scalp until it bled, then cover it with my hair so no one saw. Or I'd let myself get freezing cold and then practically burn myself in an attempt to warm up. I'd also go to bed with a hot water bottle on my stomach so hot that my stomach is now permanently burnt. But somehow those things weren't really enough. It was only a month after I hit myself again that I cut for the first time. Partly I did that to deal with some of the physical pain I was in at the time, but somehow it also made that pain a bit visible. It was also a way of expressing immense frustration. I had to pull the knife over the same bit of skin a few times before it even drew blood. But it did… and by then it was really raw and sore and so then I could cry about that and about my arm hurting instead of crying about what was upsetting me in the first place.'

JIM

'I was born in 1981, the youngest of three, to two great parents. Just before I was four we moved for my dad's job. The house was bigger, but life felt a lot harder. Dad worked hard. He was away a lot, and when he came back he was often so tired that he would have a migraine and needed to sleep. Mum went back to

uni and was away a couple of nights a week too. It was around
this time that I realized there was a lot of pain in my family. My
brother went to school, came home and went to bed and read. He
struggled to make friends, or conversation. My sister found the
schoolwork hard and worked very diligently at everything but
found life hard. Then someone told me that before my parents
knew they were expecting me they were planning to become
missionaries and move to Africa. That was what Dad and Mum
really wanted to do. I came on the scene and blew those plans
out of the water. I suddenly felt that all our pain – Dad's job,
my mum's hard time at uni, my sister's pain at school, and my
brother's social unease and fight to understand emotions – was
my fault. I knew that there were things wrong in my family, and
that there was a lot of pain, and I made it my mission to never
be any trouble, to make my life positive so it didn't add any pain
to them, and so I could be whatever was needed to make things
better.

'Then as I went through puberty I found it really hard to
sleep. Other people seem to be able to just shut their eyes and
sleep but I still cannot do that. My mind goes mental in the quiet.
Back then it would take hours to get to sleep, and in that time my
mind would be all over the place. It would think about everything
I was doing wrong and all the hurt I was causing. I tried
drowning out the thoughts with music, quoting scripture, reading
novels and with fantasies, but nothing worked.

'Eventually I started to try to literally beat the thoughts
out of my mind. I would punch my head over and over till I was
exhausted. Funnily enough that pain cut through the thoughts,
and I enjoyed the feeling of clarity, and the exhaustion that came
with it. And that is how I started to self harm.'

RACHAEL
'When I started self harming I did not actually know there was
anything out there called "Self Harm". I was at university and I
was invited to a ball one night but decided not to go last minute

because I felt fat, and that I wasn't beautiful enough to go. Instead I stayed home in my bedroom all night cutting my arms. I did not really know why I was doing it. I just hated myself.

'I did not self harm again till a few years later when I was an inpatient in a private psychiatric hospital. I saw others self harming (cutting) on the ward and I suppose I learned from them. By this stage my self harm took on two forms. I used to cut (mainly on my arms), but I also used to overdose. Sometimes this was with death in mind, but mostly it was just about trying to escape from the world or find some peace.'

LIBBY

'Self harm started when I was eleven. I discovered it by accident, and cut mainly on my arms and legs. At that stage I could manage to get away with it, telling lies to cover it up. When my mum found out she made me stand there in my underwear so she could check my body for any marks or anything. That was when I started cutting on my breasts and the top of my legs because these parts were hidden.

'I didn't just stick to cutting. I used to burn as well, and also take a lot of painkillers in one go. I did once take an overdose but I wasn't trying to kill myself. The more I learnt about different ways I could self harm the more inventive I got. Over time I learnt about "pro-self-harm" websites, which I used to visit to find new stuff out. This was also when I started messing around with my eating as I learnt more about eating disorders. I don't know if I used it to lose weight. I think it was more about the control, and was really a different form of self harm.'

2 How common is self harm and who does it?

So far we have looked at what self harm is, and shared some of the stories of four people who have experienced self harm personally. But just how common are these kinds of experiences? Probably the most talked about aspect of self harm is the way it seems to be an increasingly widespread problem. So just how many people are self harming, and who is at most risk?

It is the case with most emotional or mental health disorders, in which so many people keep their suffering secret, that it is difficult to arrive at accurate figures. Self harm is no different, and it is hard to know how close statistics we read are to accurately describing the real size of the self-harm problem. In the UK alone, self harm is known to cause around 150,000 admissions to A&E every year. In fact, the number of ten- to eighteen-year-olds admitted to hospital because of self harm over the last five years has increased by one-third. As figures suggest only just over 10–15 per cent of self-harm sufferers ever seek medical help for their wounds, this really is the tip of the iceberg.

People of all ages and backgrounds self harm, but it is most common amongst young people. The NICE (National Institute of Clinical Excellence) report into self harm states that the average age self harm starts is about twelve years old – but cases have been reported in much younger children, and hospital admissions figures show evidence that the rate of self harm in children younger than ten is increasing. For some, self harm will stop once the upheaval and challenges of adolescence have been resolved, but many sufferers continue to harm into adult life and find it impossible to stop without some form of treatment. Self harm seems to be more common in women and girls than in men and boys overall (though in fact more boys than girls under ten are admitted to hospital because of self harm). In adolescence, girls may be around two to four times more likely than boys to admit to self harm. However, it is probable that boys harm in different ways and may be more likely to cover it up as the result of an accident or a fight. Therefore, it may be that the rates in males are higher than often reported. Meanwhile, studies show that friends, and family in particular, are generally unaware that a young person is self harming.

So if self harm is most common amongst young people, then how many of them are struggling with it? Research papers looking into the size of the problem in certain places, such as schools, universities or hospitals, can give us some idea. Most agree that between 7 and 14 per cent of adolescents self harm at some stage in their life, maybe an average of about 10 per cent (so that's one in ten) at any one time. Research for the National Enquiry into Self Harm estimated that one in fifteen young people harm themselves at some stage (again, around 7 per cent). However, some of our studies in local schools have found much higher figures – with as many as 25 per cent of girls (one in four) and 12 per cent of boys admitting that they had self harmed at some point by the age of fourteen, and recent research carried out by a mental health charity in the UK found that one in three girls aged eleven to nineteen said that they had self harmed. Research also tells us that it is not unusual for teenagers to be struggling with the kinds of very powerful emotions that often trigger self harm. As many as 45 per cent (that's nearly half) admit having had suicidal thoughts at some time.

Self harm also occurs in adults, and there is some evidence that adults who self harm are at greater risk of serious consequences such as suicide attempts or hospital admission.

This may be because they represent those for whom self harm did not resolve once life settled down after adolescence, or because they are more likely to be those who self harm to cope with serious traumatic experiences or memories. Self harm may develop later in life in someone who has struggled to cope with their feelings and emotions for many years, or be triggered by a trauma or by memories of something that happened long ago. Adults who self harm have very high rates of depression and other issues such as anxiety, and for many these are chronic problems. One group of adults who seem to be at particularly high risk of self harm are those in prison. At least half of female prisoners on remand say they have self harmed at some stage in their life and over a quarter in the last year. This is most likely to be because the frequency of issues that can trigger self harm is much higher in prisoners than in the general population. Prison itself may also place them at increased risk of self harm, as they are more likely to know others who harm and are less likely to access help for other mental health problems.

One interesting fact about self harm is how knowing other people who harm seems to influence the likelihood of someone starting to harm themselves. Research done in schools has looked into the factors most likely to be associated with self harm and found that the most common one for males and females was knowing someone else who had self harmed. Many experts describe self harm anecdotally as 'contagious' or 'catching', and there are some studies that seem to back this up, showing epidemic-like patterns of self harm in hospitals and prisons. Many people who self harm describe reading or hearing about someone else who already did it, and then trying it for themselves. This would then imply that self harm is going to be increasingly likely as awareness of it spreads within a group. However, it is likely that the way many young people know about self harm today is not in fact from their friends or people they know. The vast majority of sufferers harm in secret, and although close friends may know, most people would probably not be aware of what was going on. It may well be that the increase in media attention to this issue has meant that most young people – those in the age group at greatest risk – are now well aware of what self harm is. Media coverage has a very important role in reducing the isolation that so many sufferers struggle with because they feel they are the only people doing such things to themselves. But it can carry a sting in the tail. Many who self harm admit that the first time they tried it, they did so after reading about someone else who was a self harmer.

Once self harm is known about, it does seem that it can spread, especially if there is a vulnerable group of people – and this accounts for situations in which people talk about finding 'clumps' of self harm (for example in schools or youth groups). But it is important to remember that whatever source introduces someone to self harm, it is probably their experience of the effect it has that influences their chances of continuing to harm in the future. Very few sufferers *want* to be self harming, and most have tried more than once to stop. But if this is the only way you know to deal with what you are feeling, it can be very difficult to resist the temptation to do it again.

If you want to understand what kinds of experiences and other factors make someone at risk of self harm, the most important thing is to remember where it comes from. Self harm is a strategy to cope with, express or reduce intense emotions. Therefore, it should not be surprising that it is more common if you have gone through experiences that trigger a lot of difficult and painful emotions. Any traumatic event can therefore be linked to self harm, and for someone who is recovering from self harm, such things can lead to relapse and challenge their recovery. The chance of someone self harming increases if the trauma they have experienced happened more than once – for example, in cases of abuse or domestic violence. These kinds of repeated traumatic experiences trigger very strong and painful emotions, which can often leave people struggling to cope. People who have survived this kind of distress often describe how self harm helps them to feel (temporarily) calmer and more in control. It may also provide a way to deal with distressing flashbacks and memories. Meanwhile, other factors that are linked to having problems with emotions are also often connected to self harm, including depression, anxiety, substance misuse, eating disorders and family or relationship problems. In fact, having a mental health problem such as this means you are about twenty times more likely to self harm than people who do not have any emotional difficulties.

So, there are many different issues and triggers that can lie behind any one person who is self harming, and it is very difficult to make general statements or to group sufferers together. In fact, every sufferer is unique, but it's important to remember that, whilst the reasons behind their self harm may vary, the patterns of emotion surrounding self harm are usually very similar. Self harm is not something that certain weak, strange or crazy people do. It seems to be something that almost any of us could fall into if we were in the wrong place at the wrong time, with painful emotions to deal with and no idea what to do with them. It's important to remember this – and to avoid making the mistake of labelling sufferers as different from 'normal' people. Someone who is self harming is much more than just their self harm; they are someone who has had to find a way to cope with emotions that feel out of control and totally overwhelming. Ultimately, the worst thing about self harm is that it can actually stop people from learning more helpful ways of dealing with their feelings. It provides at best a short-term solution, but one that can prove very addictive.

3 Why self harm?
PART 1: encounters with emotion

So far, what we have looked at in relation to self harm has been very much the practical reality of what it involves – the statistics, descriptions and personal experiences. But in any conversation or article about self harm, you cannot go too far without coming to the big question – and probably the most common question that we get asked: *why*? Why do people do this to themselves? Why do they find it so hard to stop? Why does it help them when they are doing something so destructive? In a way it's the most important question about self harm – for sufferers as well as for carers. If you never understand *why* you hurt yourself – what that does for you, what it is that makes you want to do that – then you are likely to struggle to get free from the problem. Without knowledge and understanding of what is going on behind the scenes of self harm, most people either carry on harming in secret or struggle with trying to stop harming through a mixture of grim determination, will power and denial – and in the end most of those people do harm again. Understanding is vital because it is the first step to being able to start sorting yourself out and moving on. It's like trying to walk through a totally dark room and finding that you keep bashing into things. It's no good just continuing to pick yourself up and try again – no matter how determined you are you will keep hitting things that you did not know were there. The first step has to be to shed some light on the situation – to start understanding what is actually going on. It is much easier to make your way on a journey when you can see where you are starting from.

The other reason that understanding is so important is that most people who self harm have a tendency to be very hard on themselves – that is, they are very prone to blaming themselves for things and tend to be very self-critical. This, combined with not understanding why they are self harming, can mean that they blame themselves. They label themselves as weak, crazy or just plain bad, and every time things get on top of them and they end up harming it seems to serve as just more proof that they are right. To them harming is something very shameful that they do that shows who they really are underneath the happy mask they try to put on for other people. It often becomes part of a wider fear that they are not the person other people think they are, and that if people find out the 'truth' they will not like them or will not want to know them. This simply isn't true (something that most sufferers will repeatedly point out to each other, but find it impossible to admit to themselves) – and realizing this is a vital stage on the route towards recovery.

The next two chapters, therefore, are about the biggest *why* – about what really lies behind self harm: why it happens and what it does to bring people temporary relief. And the best place to start is to look at how, for some people, emotions can build up and be so painful that they need to resort to strategies such as self harm in an attempt just to cope.

What are emotions?

Emotions are something that we often misunderstand and mistreat in our culture. Particularly in the UK – where we still tend to be quite reserved and try not to express our emotions too much – emotions are still treated as some kind of optional response. You will often hear people say, 'She's just far too emotional,' or 'What gives her the right to be so angry?' What we are doing when we talk – and think – like this is confusing an emotion with what we do with it afterwards – our reaction to the emotion. In fact, emotions on the whole are not voluntary. Let's imagine that I'm sitting in my living room relaxing when I hear a crash. I rush into the kitchen to find a dish broken on the floor and one of my cats sitting sheepishly next to the remains, licking up what's left of the food that was in it. Whether or not that situation triggers an emotion in me – and what emotion it is – is not something I can choose. Emotions are much more like reflex reactions than we think. So, it's as if my brain has scanned the situation and identified that the combination of elements I see before me (broken dish, dinner on floor, cat licking lips) is in some way significant to me. The emotion that results is almost like a warning flag – a type of *this may need some kind of attention/intervention* alert. That initial 'spark', or emotion, is triggered without me thinking about it or planning it.

Now what happens next is very significant. If I am at ease with my emotions, and there is no one around I am trying to impress, and I am otherwise having a reasonably good day, then with any luck I will take that spark of emotion and react simply and appropriately: swear under my breath, mutter at the cat and clean up the mess. The emotional episode will be over (see Figure 1). However, quite often what we do is

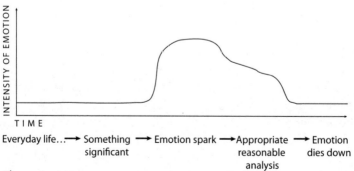

Figure 1

27

throw kindling onto that emotional spark by the way we react to it. Once we start thinking about how we are feeling, there is a significant risk that we will start to feed that flame – and we'll see the emotion grow. So, if I've had a hard day, and I am tired, and my feet are aching, and I had just sat down finally for a rest when the cat broke the bowl, then I am much less likely to react so well. I might start thinking things like 'This sort of thing always happens to me' or 'Typical – I get left to clean up the mess' or 'Can't anything go right today?', and before I know it I'll be feeling much worse. All of this doesn't take long – in fact, in the time between the crash and my finding out exactly what caused it, all those thoughts may have whizzed through my mind, taking my emotion and making it much more intense (so now I'm really cheesed off), or maybe adding/triggering other emotions (*and* I'm feeling sad because it's reminded me just how awful my day has been, *and* I'm stressed out because I never get to sit and rest…).

So, we can think of a normal emotional response in three stages. The first is that initial spark of emotion. We cannot avoid this. Even when people try to design computers that function like a human brain they find that they have to put in some kind of algorithm that mimics or is the equivalent of emotions. Life is just too complex to decide everything by rationally weighing up the pros and cons. Emotions narrow down our focus; they help us to decide what is important and what isn't; and they influence our decisions. The next stage, however, is when the emotions grow. Again, some of this we can't help. It's not my fault if I have had a bad day and the cat breaking a dish is the final straw. It's not my fault if one thing happening triggers other emotions because it brings back a painful memory. However, certain patterns of thinking or certain kinds of response can make our emotions stronger and more difficult to deal with. Then, finally, the third stage of dealing successfully with emotions rests on what we do as a result of them. Basically, we all have days in which the emotions stack up, or everything seems to be going wrong, or we're tired and vulnerable or just plain fed up. So how we deal with our emotions on those days – and on the normal days – is very important.

Why do some people struggle with their emotions?

Lots of people struggle with emotions. First of all, they can be very powerful. For some of us it is the way that we think that makes our emotions grow so strong and painful. For others it is our past experiences. Or maybe it is a bit of both. The other problem with emotions is how and when to express them. Part of experiencing any emotion is to want to *do* something: anxiety makes you want to pace or fidget; anger makes you want to hit something or yell; sadness makes you want to cry... But expressing emotions isn't always easy or appropriate. As adults many of us live and work in scenarios in which it is not always appropriate to react to every emotion immediately. Even when our children are very young we start to teach them that they need to control their emotions. But for some people *suppressing* their emotions instead of *expressing* them can become a way of life. In fact, they get so good at it that they start to not even notice those emotional sparks because they are suppressed so quickly. If this happens regularly – particularly in people whose emotions are very strong – what you end up with is a kind of bubbling pit of nasty emotions, just under the surface. These people carry their pit around with them constantly – in fact, at times they feel as though they might burst, for all their emotions are hidden. The emotions are no longer pure and understandable – linked to one incident that triggered one spark of emotion. They have grown and merged and got more complex, so that now they are very frightening and, most of all, very overwhelming. These are people who start to be at risk not just of self harm but of various things that we sometimes do in an attempt to cope with emotions that feel out of control.

The reason people resort to other strategies to try to cope is that these sorts of emotions do not tend to stay under the surface. Emotions are not designed to stay hidden – their whole purpose is to make us aware of whatever it is they were originally alerting us to – so it is hard to keep them suppressed. Eventually – typically when we are tired or lonely or our defences are down for some other reason – they will emerge. People who struggle with their emotions will often talk about being suddenly and totally overwhelmed by how dreadful they feel and how inexplicable it is – how these emotions come over them with no warning and make no sense. They feel that they are totally at the mercy of their emotions and can never rest and enjoy a 'good' day because they may, at any moment, suddenly be attacked by these horrible feelings. Once their emotions kick in, they are then prone to unhelpful patterns of thinking – perhaps the ones that made some of the emotions so strong in the first place – that serve to make their emotional pit even deeper. To be in one of these emotional chasms is utterly devastating and terribly painful. It happens to most people at some stage in their life: if life is throwing a lot at you and it just builds up too much; if something has happened that has triggered immense emotions; if you are juggling a lot of stress and a lot of change. But for some people this is a regular occurrence and a part of their everyday life. It's not too hard to understand, therefore, why they look desperately for something that helps them to cope with what is going on.

Self harm is not the only thing that people do in order to try to cope with patterns of emotion like this. In fact, these emotional build-ups are linked with many of the things that people often struggle with – alcohol and drug addiction, eating disorders, depression, anxiety problems, even post-natal depression. A lot of treatment for these conditions looks at what the emotions are that are being so problematic as well as where they are coming from. Cognitive behavioural therapy (CBT), which is recommended now as the treatment of choice for many mental health problems like these, does exactly that, focusing in particular on the unhelpful beliefs and patterns of thinking (more about these in Chapter 9) that can make emotions so much more powerful and painful.

Self harm is not a successful way of dealing with emotions. The next chapter will look at what it does and why people do find it so addictive, even though it certainly doesn't make everything better. For that reason, people struggling with self harm are also very likely to have other problems, and self harm is often something that goes on alongside something else, such as a drug or alcohol addiction, an eating disorder or a long-term problem with depression or anxiety.

If you are suffering with these problems, or caring for someone who is, then please pay close attention to the next few sentences. Struggling with emotions like these does not mean that you or anyone else who suffers in the same way are weak, crazy, bad or in any way different as a human being. What it means is that you are not coping very well with your emotions. Most likely something else is going on to intensify those emotions, which makes dealing with them even more difficult. These emotions are building up and overflowing – becoming overwhelming, and leading you in desperation to clutch at some not-very-constructive straws in a desperate attempt to cope. If this is you, then please do not be too hard on yourself. If you are feeling like this, then please get some help. You should not have to cope with feeling this bad on your own, and the risk is that you may hurt yourself seriously if you get to a stage where you cannot cope. Don't linger or think that you are just making too much of a fuss. I know you won't want to bother people, but this time it is the right thing to do. Get some help and support. If this describes someone else you are worried about, then talk to them. You will have had experiences yourself of emotions building up – it happens to everyone. So try not to focus on the self harm, which may feel totally alien to you – think about the emotions underneath. You will find yourself much more able to empathize than you may have expected.

4 Why self harm?
PART 2: *theories of self harm*

Hopefully it feels a bit clearer now why emotions and feelings can build up so powerfully that people do not know how to deal with them. The question this chapter aims to tackle is why self harm in particular seems to help, and why people find it so hard to stop using self harm to cope with their emotions even when they do want to stop. There are many different theories about self harm, just as there are many things that can trigger the emotions that go on to cause someone to want to self harm. This chapter aims to summarize the most helpful, and those that sufferers tend to identify with most strongly. They are also those that have had the most backing in research.

Triggering endorphin release
Perhaps the most interesting place to start is to look at the actual physiology of what happens when someone self harms and to understand the theories behind why people seem to find it addictive. Some neuroscientists suggest that people who self harm are inadvertently harnessing the power of natural chemicals called endorphins. Endorphins are released in the brain and act as neurotransmitters – that is, they carry chemical messages in the brain and affect the way our brains work. They have many different effects, including helping people to relax and think clearly, as well as diminishing the impact of negative emotions. Interestingly, they also seem to reduce pain and have been called the body's natural painkillers. Endorphins are strongly linked to emotions, and are associated with lots of 'feel-good' situations. It is

endorphins that are generally agreed to be the cause of what you might have heard described as a 'runner's high' – a feeling of well-being that some people experience after a long run or a hard exercise session. Some have also suggested that it is the impact of endorphin release that makes some alternative therapies such as acupuncture so effective.

Various things seem to trigger the release of endorphins – from running (or in fact any form of strenuous exercise done for long enough) to one of the chemicals found in chillies! Physical injury also triggers endorphin release, so it is possible that people who self harm are discovering the way that endorphins really do help to decrease their emotions and enable them to relax. This is especially interesting when you consider that most people typically harm in the evenings or late at night when they want to be able to calm down and get some rest. The pain-killing impact of endorphins may also explain how people are able to hurt themselves without apparent pain – although most people who self harm do feel pain and some would even say that this is a necessary part of the harming. Endorphins are certainly powerful chemicals – the 'orphin' in the name comes from their similarity to morphine – so it is theoretically possible that people are physiologically addicted to the endorphin release from self harming. However, there are some studies that question just how much this actually influences people's harming, and it is likely that it is this, combined with the psychological effects of harming, that makes it so addictive.[3]

---

3 People sometimes make it sound as if psychological addiction isn't really that important next to physical addiction. However, knowing that something will help you to feel better when the level of emotional pain is intolerable is a pretty strong motivation to do it. So it's important not to forget or play down this side of why self harm is so difficult to stop. Psychological addictions are often just as hard to break as physiological addictions – just for different reasons!

Communication

Alongside this physical factor, there are many psychological theories as to why people self harm. Of these, one of the strongest is that self harm is a way of communicating powerful emotions. When you are at the mercy of emotions that you do not understand yourself, communicating them successfully to other people can be incredibly hard. Combine this with the fact that the people who struggle the most with their emotions are often those who are the least well equipped to talk about them, and you can see that this makes communication very difficult. For most of us emotions are not easy to describe. They have as the main part of their nature something that is very difficult to put into words. How do I know that what I am experiencing right now is called 'sad'? What is it about that feeling that makes it 'sad'? It is hard to know, and most of us rely on the assumption that those we talk to about our emotions share them and therefore know what we mean (one of the reasons we are so drawn to people who seem to experience and understand the world in the same way that we do). If we feel that our emotions are out of control and way beyond what anyone else is likely to be experiencing, then it can be difficult to know whether we are successfully explaining to people how bad it is. Having a physical wound can be a kind of visible illustration of that emotional pain – much easier than putting it into words.

It's important to be clear: we are not saying that people deliberately and specifically wound themselves to illustrate what they are feeling. Self harm is more of an instinctive way of displaying that emotional pain – not just to others but to yourself as well. A physical wound can help someone validate to themselves how bad they were feeling, as well as communicate something very powerful to others. Remember, emotions have a strong component that leads us to want to do something (exactly what depends on the emotion). Some people have argued that the purpose of emotions is purely a communicative one. It follows, therefore, that for someone who is dealing with a great deal of suppressed emotion, they might instinctively do something in an attempt to communicate that. In fact, though very few people consciously aim to harm in order to communicate (most self harmers actually hide their wounds), the most common reason given for self harm is that the sufferer yearns to have people hear their pain and validate their distress – that is, to say that they understand and that it is ok to feel that way.

'Acting out' emotional responses

Another important part of most emotions is a desire to *do* something. This inclination is behind another common cause of self harm, particularly when it is tied up with feelings of frustration, anger and aggression. For some people their self harm is linked much more with these feelings than with depression or sadness. They harm out of pure frustration, hitting out and turning that emotion onto themselves. People whose self harm is linked to anger often harm in more unusual ways or do things that result in harm although that may not have been their main aim, perhaps hitting solid objects or smashing things. This form of self harm is also sometimes linked to body concerns, especially in those struggling with the emotions triggered by eating disorders or body dysmorphic disorder,[4] when sufferers may harm specific areas of their body that they dislike. In this case what is happening is that the normal tendency for the emotion to trigger an action (which can be significant if the emotion is very strong) is building up such that eventually the person does take action, but turns that action in on themselves.

---

4 Body dysmorphic disorder (BDD) is a psychological disorder in which people truly hate their physical appearance and are convinced they are ugly. This disorder causes intense distress and can lead people to become obsessive about checking their physical appearance, or to take drastic measures in an attempt to change how they look.

Anger and frustration are very powerful emotions, and it is not surprising that they can lead people to take such drastic actions, even at such a high cost.

In fact, this 'acting out' element of self harm occurs in a smaller way as part of most people's self harming. People who suffer with self harm are generally very hard on themselves, and this frustration often forms part of the trigger to want to self harm. Many sufferers will talk about how they 'deserve' to be punished, and see their self harm as something that they have brought onto themselves. It is as though they are parenting themselves in a very harsh way (some actually may have grown up under very strict parenting regimes), making sure that any little 'mistake' (whether real or perceived) results in a negative consequence. However, as we know from many studies of parenting, teaching and behaviour change, punishing bad behaviour simply isn't effective, and tends to make people sink into despair, confirming their worst suspicions about themselves and making them lose hope. These sorts of patterns of thinking are very common amongst those who self harm.

Routines and self-nurturing

People who self harm as part of an action triggered by emotion tend to do so very impulsively and without considering their behaviour for long beforehand. Another group of people, however, self harm in a much more controlled and considered way. They often have a set routine of how they harm and what they do afterwards. In part, this planning shows just how strong our natural urge to find a way to cope with emotions is. In another way, though, this can tell us something about why some people harm or what the process gives them. A lot of people who self harm struggle with caring for themselves. They may have grown up focusing on other people or being taught that they must never be selfish or lazy – and they often feel that to take time to care for themselves would be one or both. Sometimes the routine followed after self harm allows that well-earned time of self-nurturing. Self harm can also be a way of relaxing for someone who finds any other forms of relaxation difficult, forbidden or impossible. Once again, this is just normal human beings experiencing the same physical and psychological need to relax as anyone else – but finding themselves unable to meet that need another way, self harm can develop as they struggle to cope.

As a release from anxiety

Anxiety as an emotion is perhaps one of the most powerful, because for most people experiencing it is so unpleasant. In fact, research shows that some people find anxiety harder to tolerate than others – and it is these people who are more at risk of problems like self harm. If you do not like feeling anxious, then you are likely to try to do various things in order to avoid it. For example, you might try to avoid the thing that makes you anxious or perform lists of checks to make sure that you do not need to worry. When these kinds of things become a problem in themselves they become phobias or obsessive compulsive-type disorders. Many of us have to deal with anxiety on a day-to-day basis and find this very hard. Self harm can become part of a coping strategy in two main ways. First of all, it can help to stop the anxious thought patterns and cycles that can drive us mad when we are feeling anxious, as our brains seem to refuse to turn off and we keep thinking about the same things. Self harm, perhaps through the release of endorphins, helps us to relax and stop the frantic worrying. Second, self harm can provide a 'get out' clause for obsessive behaviour. For example, someone who is fighting an eating disorder and is incredibly anxious about gaining weight might force themselves to endure long exercise regimes in an attempt to deal with that level of anxiety. Self harm (or the wounds and injuries it produces) can give people the reason that they need to allow themselves to take a brief break from those unrelenting cycles of behaviour.

About dissociation

This chapter has considered many of the things that can lie at the root of self harming. One final cause that is important to mention and consider is the question of dissociation. Dissociation is a word used to describe a state of mind in which we are not consciously aware of what we are doing. Although this might sound very dramatic, in fact dissociation is not unusual and most of us do it from time to time. Think of the last time you drove your car somewhere and, having arrived, realized you could not remember most of the journey. This is a typical – and normal – example of dissociation. Dissociation is something that people may do in order to cope with strong emotions or intense physical pain. People will sometimes talk about traumatic experiences and say that they do not remember them or that they were 'out of it' at the time. Often they are referring to the impact of dissociation. Most people agree that self harmers must dissociate to some degree – without being able to separate themselves from the physical pain involved they would not be able to do it. Some even suggest that this dissociation – cutting them off emotionally as well as physically – is part of what makes self harm feel effective, as it distances that person from the emotions they are unable to cope with.

However, for some people who self harm dissociation is a much more serious problem. Children, who have a much less stable identity and are still forming an idea of who they are, are much more able to dissociate than adults (something we see in a harmless form in their ability to form make-believe worlds so easily). If children experience pain or trauma – particularly if that is repeated – they may learn to dissociate in order to escape it. Someone who has used dissociation to cope with emotion in this way since they were young, or someone who encountered something so distressing in their adult life that they had to dissociate in order to cope, may well find that they start to have problems with dissociation. Some find that certain memories – or even smells, sounds or occurrences that remind them of traumatic events – can push them into a dissociative state without them realizing it. They may feel detached from what they are doing, have trouble concentrating or even lose patches of time in which they do not remember what they did. The risk that people will be injured and the distressing nature of what happens can make dissociation a serious psychological disorder. Dissociation can be part of a problem with self harm because people may harm in order to bring themselves back to full awareness, or they may harm when not in control of what they are doing.

Problems with dissociation are very complex and usually need expert treatment. If you or any people you know who self harm are struggling with periods of dissociation, please seek help, particularly if you are experiencing times when you are unaware of what you are doing. This is really important for your own protection as well as for those around you. It is often linked with some notable or severe trauma and is likely to need significant therapy with someone who is experienced in these kinds of issues. It should not be taken lightly.

5 First steps in getting help for self harm

The first few chapters in this book have talked about what self harm is – who does it and why. But the aim of this book is not to focus on self harm; it is to focus on how to start working towards recovery! This chapter is a practical guide to taking those first steps towards getting formal help, starting with a look at the different options that are available to you if you are seeking help, either for yourself or for someone you care about who is self harming.

First steps

First and foremost it is essential that the person seeking help really wants it. This may sound obvious, especially if you are the one supporting a sufferer. Why would anyone not want help to stop hurting themselves? But do remember that self harm is complicated: it is a strategy that helps people feel in control and helps them to cope with feelings that are otherwise very frightening. Try not to rush people into getting help. It is important that the person you are trying to support feels cared for, not pushed into help that they are not even sure they want. If you are seeking help for yourself, well done! It's not an easy step to take. It's worth taking a moment to think about the main reasons why you want to stop self harming, and why you are starting to look for help. You could perhaps write them down, or chat to a friend or therapist about them (see Chapter 6 for more on working out *why* you want to stop). It's important to know why you are setting out on a journey – especially when it might not be that easy. Don't risk starting without ever really thinking about why you are leaving!

When people start to look for help for self harm – or any emotional/psychological problem – they often feel very keen to get started as quickly as possible. Most people would admit that what they are looking for at this point is, ideally, a magic wand or pill that will make things immediately (or very quickly) much better. Try to be realistic! Most people who self harm have spent many, many years perfecting the patterns of thinking and emotion that are involved, and then expect to be able to change them in a matter of weeks. Remember that you may need to be a bit more patient. Also, remember that you, or the sufferer, know the details of what is going on really well, but the people you ask for help do not. You may need to bear with them at first, because often getting the right help requires several appointments and lots of questions. The people you see may even want you to show that you really do want to get better. If they think there is a chance that maybe you were pushed into seeking help, just aren't sure, or need a bit more time, then they are likely to comment on this. This isn't because they think you are wasting their time, or are too mad/bad/crazy to be helped, or anything else; it's just because you have a much better chance of responding well to treatment if you really do want to get better. They may want to wait a few weeks to get an idea of what your self harm is like. They may well also want to spend some time chatting with you; treatment is likely to involve quite a lot of talking about what is going on for you and why, so they need to make sure that you are ready and able to do that. Try to be patient through this stage. Frustrating as it might seem, and hard as it is to try to explain yourself to someone else when part of the whole problem is that you don't entirely understand why you do it, do your best. It's about helping them to help you.

WHERE TO GO FOR HELP

Although there are other people who can refer a sufferer for help, the best place to start is usually with your GP.[5] They have a wide range of routes that they can direct you down, as well as hopefully having a breadth of knowledge about the services available within the NHS. Really good GPs will also know about what voluntary or support groups are running locally. Remember that to them self harm is probably not what they see as the main problem. They may see it as a symptom of something else that is going on underneath. They will want to check whether you struggle with other things such as anxiety or depression, and they may want to try to treat these first – before looking at the self harm. This may not be what you were expecting – but remember, if they can help you to decrease the level of difficult emotion you are struggling with it will make working on the self harm much easier. Self harm can't be treated on its own – it's always important to look at what it is helping you to cope with as well.

BE PREPARED!
Before you visit the GP, do some preparation. Don't just go in and try to explain it all off the top of your head. A large proportion of your GP's work will be about mental health issues, so they should be used to talking about them, but you may not be! Before you go, think about what you want to say. You may want to make a list of the key points so you can refer back to them and make sure nothing has been missed (see box). Try to be concise and avoid rambling (though we all do that sometimes!). The list will help you to do that, and to feel confident afterwards that you handled it well.

As you talk to the GP, they may just listen quietly, or they may ask questions or want you to clarify certain things. After you've had a chance to talk, they should explain what they would recommend for you, and what actions they would like

5 Although referrals generally come from GPs, other people can refer you, such as hospital consultants and school SENCOs (Special Educational Needs Co-ordinators).

Topics you might want to cover when talking to your GP:

- When you first harmed

- What was going on then

- How often you harm

- What it is you do when you harm

- How you feel before and after you harm

- Anything you know of that is contributing to your harming or that triggers the urge to harm

- Any other feelings, thoughts or behaviours that worry you (such as suicidal thoughts or painful emotions/memories)

- Any other symptoms (such as trouble sleeping or anxiety)

to take. This is your chance to ask any questions and share any concerns, so do be honest. There is no point in them prescribing pills if you know you have no intention of taking them, for example, so talk to them about your worries. You may be fighting a desire to just get it over with as quickly as possible and get out of the room, but stick with it. You'll be frustrated later if you don't take the chance, so take a deep breath and make sure you have said the things you wanted to. Whatever they suggest, whoever they refer you to, remember that your GP should be the main source of support. They should know you and listen to you and coordinate any other care you are getting, so get to know them and make sure they understand where you are coming from.

If you are struggling with self harm yourself, do think about taking someone with you on this first difficult trip to see the GP. It is very common for people to freeze when they face a stranger to discuss their self-harming behaviour, and sometimes having another person there can give you extra confidence and ensure you actually go through with it. It also means they can talk with you before you go about what you want to say, and offer prompts if necessary, or even help you to explain things to the doctor. Your GP will be happy to have someone in with you if that's what you want.

WHAT IF IT DOESN'T GO TO PLAN?
In writing all this we have assumed that the GP you see is up to date, alert, helpful, a good communicator and an all round nice person! However, sometimes people don't have such a good experience with their GP. This is another reason why having someone else with you can be really valuable, because then you have another perspective on what happened. If you don't get the response you had hoped for, don't despair. Most surgeries have more than one GP you can talk to, so perhaps try another at a different time. Ultimately, there is nothing to stop you changing your GP if you cannot get the support you need. But hopefully you'll have better luck with another GP. Speaking of timing, it's worth being aware that GPs are still under a lot of time pressure when seeing patients. Most good GPs are flexible and will be able to give you the time you need. But don't panic if they stop you and suggest that you come back another time to discuss things more fully. They are simply making sure that they can give you enough time. To avoid this some practices will allow you to book a double appointment, so think about asking the receptionist when you call.

The next step
Once you have been to see your GP the chances are you will be referred on for extra help. This will come from some form of mental health service – which kind depends on how old you are. Child and Adolescent Mental Health Services (CAMHS) provide interventions for those aged under eighteen. They often deliver a vast range of therapies – art therapy, music therapy, play therapy, counselling, psychotherapy, family

therapy and so on. If you are referred when you are not far off eighteen, and it seems likely that the support needed will be for longer than the remit of CAMHS, you may be referred to Young People's Services (YPS), an agency that straddles the child and adult services, to help with the transition from one to the other. The YPS is more of an adult service, but it is presented in a form that makes it accessible to younger adults. If you are over eighteen, referrals will be made directly to the adult Mental Health Service (MHS), which may be community-based or clinic-based.

Whatever service you are referred to, you are likely to start off with an assessment appointment, generally with a psychologist, psychiatrist or CPN (community psychiatric nurse). The purpose of this appointment is to decide which support is most appropriate. On the whole, if self harm is specifically mentioned, then the initial assessment should take place within a month or so of the referral being made, although waiting lists can mean that it takes longer. Don't be afraid to ask how long the wait is likely to be. Following this there may be another wait for further treatment – which will usually be offered as outpatient care, although in some cases (for example, if you are already in hospital because of your injuries, or if you are felt to be at risk of very serious injury) inpatient care will be suggested.

About drugs and medication

One issue that often comes up when seeking treatment is that of whether to take medication or not. As part of your treatment for self harm, especially if you are also struggling with depression or anxiety, you may find that it is suggested that you try taking some antidepressant medication. A lot of people instinctively and immediately don't want to, but before you shut the book and move on to something else, you need to understand why these drugs are prescribed. There are two main reasons. First of all, antidepressant medication can, of course, help you to deal with feelings of depression and anxiety that can underlie difficult emotions. That is one reason it may be prescribed. Another, less commonly known reason is that some antidepressants can help people to deal with the obsessive patterns of thinking that can accompany difficult emotions (especially anxiety). Therefore, they can really help people to stabilize self harm and keep safe whilst other treatment is going on. Most people do not want to take antidepressants; they feel that they want to work out the cause of their problems, not just take a pill for the rest of their life. But actually, antidepressants should not be prescribed in that way anyway. Antidepressants will not solve your problems on their own, but it's important not to rule them out. They can help to keep things steady whilst you wait for referrals and to think more clearly whilst you are starting to work on recovery, and they can take some of the sting out of your emotions, giving you a chance to start working through them. Imagine it like this: sometimes struggling against problems like self harm can be a bit like trying to get across a lake in a boat with a hole in it. You have to work very hard constantly bailing out water so that you don't go under and this can be exhausting. In fact, bailing is so hard that you can't work on plugging the hole that is causing the problems in the first place! Medication won't fix the hole, but what it does do is pump the water out for you so that you don't have to bail so hard – meaning that then you can start to work on fixing the hole.

Make sure your GP also refers you for some other help, but be aware how medication might help you to cope and to respond to other 'talking' therapies more effectively. Studies have shown that depression is under-treated in those who self harm, so don't miss out on something that could help.

NB: If you know that you or the person you are caring for has struggled with suicidal thoughts, or that you sometimes take too many drugs as part of self harm, don't be afraid to ask your GP to prescribe antidepressants on a week-by-week basis. This is not unusual and is a simple precaution.

About seeking emergency care for self harm

As well as seeking treatment and referrals from a GP, some sufferers may need to seek emergency treatment for their injuries – and for some it is from A&E that they are referred for extra support.

You may have heard stories about people being treated badly when they go to A&E with self-induced wounds. Sadly, these things can happen, but it's important to remember that positive stories don't get nearly as much attention. If you have to go to A&E to get help, remember that every patient should be treated with respect and dignity, regardless of their reason for checking in to the hospital. As with any injury, the medical staff there will question you about how it happened. If you admit it was self harm, they have to offer the opportunity for you to see the duty psychiatrist. It is up to you whether you refuse or accept this offer, but it can be another route towards getting some help. If you do need to go to A&E and find it a very daunting prospect, remember that you do not have to go alone. The NICE guidelines state that you should have the choice as to whether you have a friend or family member to support you. They also state that practices such as denying anaesthesia for stitching are wholly unacceptable. Don't be afraid to stand up for yourself. It is now agreed to be completely wrong to treat a self harmer in a way that just triggers more pain and that suggests a lack of dignity. If you do have a bad experience, remember there are complaints procedures you can follow to make sure it is looked into so that other people do not have to suffer in the same way.

If you have been to A&E and turned down any extra help,

but now would like some more support, remember that every A&E visit usually results in a letter or email being sent to the patient's GP (if you do see a psychiatrist, they will also write), so your GP will be aware of what has happened. You may want to follow up an A&E visit by dropping in to see your GP to chat about what happened. Once again, take someone with you if you think that this will help. Even if you are getting help and support from other people, your GP remains the person who should coordinate that support and make sure you are cared for appropriately. So use them well, and give them the chance to get to know you and understand what is going on.

Real-life experiences…

Once it had started, how did your self harm develop?

NINA

'I carried on self harming. It was usually late at night when I cut. I was usually crying and felt there was no one to talk to. I was feeling lonely, vulnerable, as if I'd never be able to cope with life and as if no one could see the mess on the inside of my life. In some ways recovering from an eating disorder made that worse. I'd put weight on, and so to the people who had been concerned about me, my outer shell wasn't showing that I was a mess inside any more in the same way as being thin had. They thought I was better but I wasn't. Probably I was getting more and more depressed, but I'm stubborn and I didn't want to talk to the GP because I assumed he'd put me on antidepressants and that (wrongly) felt as if it would be the ultimate in failure. So I kept trying to cope myself.

'In a strange way the self harm made me feel more alone. I couldn't tell anyone what I was doing – I guess I was too embarrassed or too proud or too scared to say. And yet it also gave me a protective kind of cocoon of safety – something I could retreat into, something I could think about, that no one else knew about, and in that way it was very addictive. When I felt bad during the day or vulnerable when I was out with people, I'd think about how I could hurt myself later, or I'd slip off and look at what I'd already done and somehow it made me feel better or reassured. I'd cut and then pick at it, making it bleed every day for weeks on end, until I got scared, covered it up and began to let it heal. Even then I found it satisfying to see the scars.

'It was also addictive because it was a way of communicating, though I wasn't actually using it to communicate to anyone else because I kept it hidden. But it kind of communicated to me that I was having a really hard time. I often felt that my problems

weren't valid – that I should be able to cope with both my physical and emotional pain better, and that the problems I had weren't as bad as other people's and so I shouldn't be making a fuss anyway. Cutting kind of represented all those feelings and made them a bit real.

'In hindsight I also think that it was partly to do with not really having much idea how to express any negative emotions, particularly anger. I was good at looking after other people or listening to them, but not very good at expressing myself, letting them look after me or looking after myself.'

JIM

'I never told anyone about my self harming. I knew that I needed help, but I couldn't tell anyone because it would cause people worry and pain. The punching continued, with me sometimes punching myself, and sometimes punching the bed or furniture. Then I began cutting myself, and that too felt good in a weird way.

'I would cut myself to express my pain. I would cut myself to express the pain that I was causing to others around me. I would cut myself out of detached interest about how deep I could cut, and I would cut to watch the blood. I began wearing long-sleeve tops and told no one. Sleep came when I cut myself and cried myself to sleep. My mind got darker and darker, so that when I cut myself I also hoped that by accident I might go too far and die.

'Then I got beaten up coming back from a party, and sleeping got even harder. The pain would keep me up, but I tried not to complain. I didn't tell anyone about the attack, and made the other person who was with me not tell anyone either. My dad told me that every now and then as a baby when I couldn't sleep he would dip his finger into some whiskey and put it on my lips, and it soothed me. I started drinking whiskey to get to sleep. It started out as small amounts and then grew till I was drinking a couple of shots each night. Cutting also continued, and I still told no one. And that gave me significance. I was different, and I didn't need to tell anyone about it.

'I knew I needed help, but didn't know how to word it, or ask for it. My mind got more and more fragmented. I used to cycle a lot, and began using cycling to punish myself, pushing myself harder and harder. I also felt that this gave God an excuse to kill me. I would cycle over hills in pitch black, and hope that I would have an accident. The exercise helped, and sometimes it would exhaust me enough that I would sleep.'

RACHAEL

'In the end I was an inpatient several times over the next year, often staying in for months at a time. Whilst I was in the psychiatric hospital I continued to self harm. Over this time my self harm became progressively worse as I learnt new ways of cutting and as my overdosing reached new levels of seriousness. I was overdosing multiple times in one week and this meant I was in and out of hospital. Often on leaving hospital I would take another overdose and land straight back in hospital again. Sometimes I would even ingest pills whilst under the care of A&E. Eventually I was able to see a psychiatrist, and he diagnosed me with depression and anxiety. I was offered cognitive behavioural therapy and began treatment.

'I think for me self harm was a way of coping with emotions that I classed as unmanageable. It was my way of running away from and avoiding my feelings. I did not think at this time that I could cope with the feelings I had. I think my self harm was linked to my depression but also I think it began to meet needs in me that were not being met or had not been met in my childhood. By cutting or overdosing I was getting attention in the form of treatment but also from family and friends as they worried and fussed round me. At the same time there were other things that kept me self harming. I liked the buzz that I got when I cut; I liked to see blood because I liked to see that I was causing myself pain. I suppose this was linked to the fact that I hated myself, and the more I self harmed, the more that self-loathing increased, as I just gave myself more reasons to hate myself, if that makes sense. The *scars and wounds were very important to me. If my wounds got close to healing then I knew I needed to do some damage again.'*

LIBBY

'As my self harm developed, a lot of my time was taken up with thinking of new ways that I could self harm or different things I could use. I think I liked to push myself as far as I could sometimes. I found taking the painkillers easier because they left no marks, so it was easier to hide. I didn't really feel that I had to cut when I was sad or I felt a certain emotion. To me it felt like I just had to do it when I had to do it. It didn't matter where I was or what I was doing; I guess it was an addiction. The older I got the more I understood what I was doing and what implications it would have for me. There was a point when I didn't think I was ever going to stop.

'I don't remember telling my parents the second time. I think my mum just knew; she was far more involved than my dad, who just stuck his head in the sand. She blamed herself for everything and kept telling me she was a bad mother and it was her fault, which sometimes made matters worse for me. She didn't understand very well that it wasn't because of her or anyone in the house: it was just me. For a while my siblings didn't know anything, as they were quite young at the time. They were kept a lot in the dark about it until we had to go to family counselling. It took over our family life, and my mum hid razors and anything sharp from me; I could see her always looking at me to see if she could see any marks. All trust in me was gone. My mum now says that at that stage whenever she walked into the house she worried about what she was going to find.'

Part 2

Recovering from self harm

6 Recovery: making a good start

Part 1 of this book has looked at self harm with the help of statistics, research, theories and some personal experiences. But in this second part of the book we'll be focusing on what is really the most important aspect of self harm: how to make a start towards working on recovery.

Recovery from self harm *is* possible

When you are trying to work through any mental health-related problem, there is always a fear in the back of your mind that maybe you will never recover, and that perhaps there is just something wrong with you that is causing you to do what you do. This just isn't the case where self harm is concerned. You are reacting to difficult and painful emotions, and self harm has developed as you struggle to cope with them. Working through those feelings, understanding them better and looking at the thought patterns and issues that are linked with your self harm *will* help you to start to recover.

This doesn't mean that recovery happens overnight. We all want to be able to change ourselves as quickly as possible if we are doing something we'd rather stop! But the reality is that if you are going to achieve real, long-term recovery, it takes time. Don't rush yourself or be too harsh with yourself if you feel things are moving too slowly. Self harm is the strategy you have relied on to cope with your feelings – sometimes for a very long time. Recovery is not just about stopping harming; it is about finding something else you can do to deal with how you feel, as well as working through some of those feelings. Give yourself time!

Don't try to go it alone

It's always tempting to try to work on recovery on your own. Because so many people struggle with feeling ashamed of their self harm, a lot try to get over it without any outside help. Remember that self harm is nothing to be ashamed about. Although you may wish that you could keep it to yourself and just get over it, most people do need some support and help as they work towards recovery. Think about who you can share this journey with. Recovery is not easy, and there are likely to be times when an outside opinion could make all the difference. For a lot of people, breaking that cycle of secrecy is a really significant step. Perhaps think about a friend you could share your story with, and lend them a copy of this book. Or maybe there is a leader, teacher, therapist or colleague you can ask for help.

Know why *you* want to stop

When you are starting to think about recovery, the first step is to decide that you do want to stop. This may sound obvious, but a lot of people rush headlong into trying to change without ever really thinking about *why*. If it is you who are harming yourself, it must be *your* decision to want to get well. If you don't want to stop, if you are doing it for someone else, or if you simply aren't sure and feel pushed into it, the chances are you will struggle much more with recovering. Think about it this way: if a smoker feels he should give up but isn't really motivated and isn't actually doing it for himself, then how do you think he will react in that moment when he is all alone and actually *really* fancies a smoke? Ultimately, the person this affects is you: it's your life, your body and your future. And the only person who will definitely be there when you feel the urge to harm is *you*! So it's best to have that person (you!) fighting on your side.

A lot of friends and relatives who find self harm really distressing and desperately care for the person suffering will say things like 'Do it for me!' or 'Please, I just wish you would stop doing something that upsets me so much.' This attitude, whilst well meaning and totally understandable, really isn't helpful. The most important thing if you are working on recovery is that you don't feel set up to fail – that is, that you don't become tied up in guilt and shame over the effect your harming has on someone else. Trying to stop self harming for someone else does this and can trigger a real fear of 'failure' for letting that person down. I've put 'failing' in inverted commas, because often people feel that if they ever harm again after saying they will try to recover, this is 'failing'. But of course it isn't. Recovery doesn't mean stopping harming just like that. If it were that simple you certainly wouldn't need to be reading this book! But trying to stop for the sake of someone else puts you in a position in which any time you harm it does feel like a failure. So that pressure really isn't helpful.

By the way, lots of sufferers feel under pressure like this even though the people who are supporting them never said anything about stopping. It's as if deciding to try to quit brings out the fear and all the questions in your mind about whether you will ever really be free, and that – combined with the fact that you really don't want to be upsetting people you care for – can make you feel you are letting everybody down. Some people even find that their harming gets worse as soon as they decide to try to stop. It's as though the fear of letting people down becomes a self-fulfilling prophecy, and the pressure resting on you can become overwhelming in itself. If this happens to you, don't panic. You need to take some time, preferably with someone to help you, to look at your fears and the pressure you feel under. Those thoughts are natural – and somehow they are always more scary in your mind than when talked over with a friend or therapist. Just remember, one important fact about recovery is that you need to be doing it for *you*! Another is that recovery *is possible*.

Yes, even for you. You just need to believe in it and not lose hope.

So take some time right now to think about that decision to recover. The choice to recover is very poignant: it signifies someone retaking control of their life; it shows motivation and commitment. Get a piece of paper and draw on it a table with two headings – 'pros' and 'cons'. Then write down as many of the pros and cons of your self harm as you can think of. Try to be thorough – you can include things other people would want you to include, but make sure you include your own ideas too! Don't shy away from admitting the positives. If it makes you feel more in control, write that down. If it helps you to feel calmer, put it on the list. It's important you do this thoroughly so you know you were not cheated and that you made this decision for yourself. Try in the same way not to gloss over any of the cons. Is not being able to wear short sleeves *really* no big deal? Does the amount you spend on plasters and bandages *really* not bother you? When you think you have finished, think ahead five years. If you were to continue to harm, would there be any pros or cons then that you didn't think of for now? For example, perhaps right now you are not that worried about scarring. But if you continue to harm, in a few years it might be a much bigger concern. Add anything like this to your list. You might want to put longer-term issues in a different colour to make it clear that they are things that don't affect you now but would in the future.

Take as much time as you can to do this list. You may want to leave it on your desk or in your diary over a few days or even a week so that you can add things to it when you think of them. Don't feel under pressure to rush this step – it is the foundation you will build your recovery on. When you have finished, take some time to look at it. Here is when that friend or person supporting you can be really helpful – spend some time with them chatting about what you wrote. Did anything surprise you? Which bits did you find easy to write down and which bits hard?

Looking at the list, can you summarize now why you want to recover? Try to write a paragraph that explains the positive side as well as the negative. It might read something like this:

> *'For me, cutting helps me to feel more in control and gives me something I can do when I feel overwhelmed and really sad. But I know that in the long run it won't help me deal with what makes me sad and I don't want to keep having wounds and scars that I need to hide. I don't like being someone who has to cut to keep going and I want to be able to be truly happy. That's why I want to recover and leave it behind.'*

When you have managed to write the paragraph, copy it onto a card and put that card somewhere you will see it – maybe on a wall or stuck to your fridge or mirror, or in your diary. You might want to keep a copy in your purse or back pocket so you can refer to it when things get hard. You could also add other inspiring things you have read, heard or that people have said to you. Some people find it helpful to start a sort of recovery-focused diary, in which they write down things they have heard, seen or thought of that help inspire them to keep working on recovery. Remember, this is about building your recovery on a solid foundation. It's worth taking some time over and it's worth continuing to build it up.

About other people's expectations, and how to set good goals

Of course, even once it is clear in your mind why you want to recover, that doesn't make you immune to other people's expectations and pressures. I often hear people I am working with saying things like 'But my friend so and so says I should be doing better by now!' or 'My mum says that now I am better I should be happy!' Sometimes our friends, relatives or even random people whom we barely even know can say things to us that have a huge impact, even if they were only meant as throwaway comments. But remember, these people are not experts. They may know nothing at all about self harm, or depression, or anxiety, or whatever it is you are trying to deal with. Don't give them more authority than they deserve!

Trying to avoid taking other people's opinions too seriously is important because most sufferers put quite enough pressure on themselves. Often when you are so keen to change things you try to push yourself too fast – and then when things don't work out as you had hoped it can feel really dreadful. It's much better to take things slowly, one step at a time. Think about trying to change any kind of behaviour. If we're honest, we often expect to be able to rid ourselves completely of a habit or behaviour in one easy move. We want to be perfect straight away. When we then slip up in any tiny way, we feel as though we've failed, and if we're not careful, we can give up the whole attempt. Often it isn't really failure – it's just that the goal was set too high.

So how might this affect the way you think of recovery? Many people faced with someone who is self harming try to get them to agree that they won't do it any more. Just like that – no help, no other strategies to deal with how they are feeling – just sheer will and determination to never harm again. Are you surprised that those sufferers almost always end up harming again? So try to avoid the often well-meaning promises to 'never harm again', or, if you are a carer, reassure the person you are supporting that you do not expect them to change overnight. Recovery is a process, little by little, one step at a time towards a different reality. Don't try to do it all at once. Remember that at first little changes are big changes. The root of self harm is its use as a coping strategy –

someone who self harms does so in order to cope with things that they otherwise wouldn't know how to handle. Recovery must involve a process of identifying what those things are, changing patterns of emotion and strategies for coping with them, and perhaps examining some past experiences and considering what they have made you think about yourself. It is normal whilst working on recovery to find that at difficult times the urge to harm gets stronger, even when you thought you were doing really well at recovery and had not harmed for ages. This does not mean you were not on the road to recovery or that you have 'backslidden' or failed. It just means that something has happened that has triggered your old strategy to cope. Episodes like this can be very important because they can teach you what you use self harm for, and each one can make you stronger in the long run.

Delaying harming

One excellent starting point is to aim to delay harming. This can be a great first step when avoiding it completely is too big a jump. It works because on the whole self harm is a short-term, impulsive coping strategy. If you can develop the skill of waiting a short time before harming, you may find that this reduces how often you harm and how severe it is if you do. This is also a great way to start to introduce other strategies for dealing with emotions or changing your thinking (see Chapters 8 and 9). Try to brainstorm a list of things that you can do to delay your harming for just a short period of time – maybe up to half an hour. The best strategies involve getting you out of the room you are in (particularly if this is where you usually harm), making contact with someone else (reducing isolation) and/or doing activities that are very mentally absorbing. Things you find relaxing are also great because relaxation neutralizes negative emotions and the physical changes that go with them. So try calling a friend, popping out to post a letter or watching half an hour of funny TV. Think about taking a bath, listening to some calming music, or reading a book or magazine. Try to compile as long a list as possible of things you can do. Get your friend or those supporting you to help. What do they do when they feel low or need to cheer themselves up or relax? Add those ideas to the list.

Once you have your list, put it somewhere safe. Then the next time you feel the need to harm, choose one to try. Don't rule them out before you even try them because you think they won't work. Give it a go for at least ten minutes. Remember that this is a start – it's not a solution to your harming – so do not rely on this to solve the whole problem, or feel too down if you do end up harming anyway. You may find that at times this really helps, and introducing these things into your life will help you to be more calm and generally deal with emotion better. Even if you don't find the urge to harm goes completely, you might find it lessens. Make a note of what works and what doesn't; that way you are starting to look at alternative ways to cope with how you are feeling.

We hope that these first steps help you to make a good start on recovery. They are really about helping you to get your harming a bit more under control, and keeping you safe so that you have the time and energy to look at some of the other issues involved. They are just the start! Reducing harming and moving away from it as a coping mechanism can only be effective if the underlying issues are realized and dealt with – and that's what we'll move on to next.

7 How to start reducing self-harming behaviour

Once they have made the decision to work on recovery, it's natural that the first thing most people long to see is a change to the way they self harm. Most want to see it happening less, or at the very least, things getting better.

At this point it's worth talking briefly about the way that the recovery process tends to work. Obviously, recovery is about getting better in the long term. However, some people will find that when they first start getting treatment or therapy, things do seem to get harder. This happens for two reasons. The first is that sometimes things you have kept pushed well down in your mind for a very long time are starting to come to the surface. This can be really hard and can in itself trigger more emotions that you would usually deal with by harming. The second reason is that asking for help and starting to try to work on recovery is a really frightening step to take. A lot of people find that the fear of failing – of this not working out and them ending up back at square one – is very hard to cope with. Many sufferers have had bad experiences in the past in which they have tried to stop and not succeeded, or where other people have tried to help them, but failed. If you are struggling with these fears, don't do it alone. Talk to those supporting you and don't be afraid of what you are feeling – it is totally natural. What you want to avoid is that fear actually being the stumbling block to recovery. Sometimes the fear can trigger a self-fulfilling prophecy – people fear they may never recover, so they worry they will harm more, which creates lots of difficult emotions that they can't deal with... so in the end they do harm more.

Try not to get caught in this cycle. Remember that recovery is about the long term, not what happens this week, or next week. It's about next year, the years after – about what you want to do with your life long term. This is also the reason why getting good support and professional guidance is really important. In those early stages of recovery you will find having someone to take those fears to invaluable.

Factors involved in the urge to harm

If you want to reduce your self harm you need to think practically as well as look at the underlying issues (more on these in the chapters that follow). There are three things involved when a person starts to feel that urge to harm: chemical release, habit and overwhelming emotion. We'll look at emotions in the next chapter, so let's consider the other two factors now:

CHEMICAL RELEASE

As we've already talked about (see Chapter 4), when someone self harms it releases a rush of chemicals into the bloodstream called endorphins. Endorphins are the body's natural opiates and can be addictive. The body produces them when there has been an injury. Amongst other effects, they make you feel an unnatural sense of calm and release from the injury and also from whatever it was that led to the injury. This physiological system has been suggested as something that lies at the root of self harm: sufferers are harnessing this calming effect of injury to help them find release from difficult emotions, relax and switch off.

So how can you use this knowledge to help you improve your chances of reducing your harming? Looking for another way to trigger endorphins doesn't work because any alternatives are either just as addictive as self harm or totally unreliable. No, what our knowledge about the role of endorphins teaches us is that we need to learn and practise some other ways of achieving the same relaxation, and of getting rid of negative feelings.

Relaxation is a bit of a foreign subject for a lot of people. Very few parents deliberately teach their children how to relax and deal with stress. In fact, most parents have never been taught how to do it either! But we live in such a stressful world now that it really is an important tool for coping with modern life. After all, most emotional reactions produce physical changes that, in the long run, can lead us to become chronically stressed if we don't relax regularly.

So think about what you do to relax. If you're amongst the people who never do anything to relax, you need to change your behaviour! Some people seem to think that relaxing is for wimps. But the reality is that the human body was not designed to work solidly; it was built to function best when periods of work and stress are interspersed with time to wind down. Every human should do something relaxing every day for at least half an hour. So unless you are arguing that you are not a human, that includes you! In fact, in stressful times (which includes when you are working on recovery) or when you have had a particularly bad day, you may find it helpful to schedule in something longer.

All kinds of activities can be relaxing, so try to be creative with what you try. Think about the people you know well. What kinds of things do they do to relax? The most important thing is that you are doing something regularly that helps you to relax; this will reduce the chance of your needing to use self harm to produce the same effect. So, go back to your list of things that you can try to delay harming from Chapter 6. Can you add some things to that list that are there just because they are relaxing? Now, don't wait until you have the urge to harm; try to get there before that stage by planning something for every day. Think of your body as being a bit like a bank account – you can't keep taking things out if you never put anything back in!

HABIT

Self harm is a strategy that you have developed to help you cope with difficult emotions. Are you bored of reading that yet? It is so key to the way you need to understand self harm that we will say it again and again. One potential weakness we have as humans is that we tend to go with what we already know – and doing something new is always harder than doing what we've always done. This means that if you grew up in abusive relationships, you may find yourself getting into more abusive relationships once you're an adult. It's not nice, but it is what you know and a pattern that is strangely hard to break out of. In the same way, if self harm is what you do to cope with things, it will take you some time to overcome that habit and move on to something else – even if that something else is much more positive and is something you really do want to do.

Never underestimate the power of the routine you have when you harm. In fact, the more of a routine you follow, the more this may be an issue. Some people have more of an established routine to their harm than others. There may be regular times when they harm, ways they harm, places they harm and so on. Their daily routine will be dotted with reminders – places they have harmed, items that have been used for harm before, memories of times when they last harmed. These kinds of things can often generate dozens of triggers for the harmer. If you don't take this into account when trying to change your harming behaviour you will find it much harder. Think about the stages you go through in your harming routine. Can you move the things that might remind you of it and push you into the early stages? Think about what triggers your harming routine and what you can do to make this less likely.

Explaining how you can change your routine is difficult, so let's look at an example. Imagine you have just given up caffeine. Now, every time you go into a coffee shop you find yourself overcome with a desire for a nice strong latte or a cappuccino. Even though you had good reasons for giving up the caffeine in the first place you might be at risk of slipping up. You have lost part of your routine and instinctively want to return to it. The best way to deal with this is to change your routine – so go somewhere else instead of coffee shops, or find something else to drink whilst you're there. In the same way, sometimes you can replace elements of your self-harm routine with other things that are positive – that is, activities that you enjoy and that help you to relax and take your mind off self harm.

Replacing habits with other actions eventually starts to create new habits and a new sense of normality. So, if you have the urge to harm and you know that the minute you walk into your room you will go to where your harming kit is kept and set up to harm, think about introducing another step instead and practise it. Maybe the first thing you will do is go in, make a cup of tea and call a friend. Again, you can look back at the list of things to do to delay harming that you compiled in Chapter 6. Try to change your routines and put in things that are positive rather than negative. A good option is to develop habits around things you enjoy. So, maybe when you get in from work you could always make a cup of tea and read the paper for twenty minutes, or perhaps do something else you enjoy. Be aware of how routine and habit can make it harder to stop and don't be afraid to do some things differently.

Sometimes habits can be about how self harm helps to meet certain needs you have at the time. Maybe you feel out of control and need something to help calm you down or to distract you from the way you are feeling. Some people who follow a very rigid and step-by-step pattern may actually find that the routine stage of the harm calms them as much as the harming. If this is you then think about other things you can do to help you feel more in control. Try sorting out a cupboard or tidying a room – anything that restores order. Some people even find ironing or washing up helpful! Or look for things that involve following a strict plan, such as baking, and get you thinking about patterns and structure – puzzles, or even learning a new language. If you are trying to distract yourself from your emotions, remember that part of their purpose is to get your attention – so, to be successful in moving your focus away, you need to find something that takes 100 per cent of your concentration. Try something absorbing such as logic problems, learning a musical instrument or even playing computer games.

About harm minimization

A lot of the things we are talking about in this section of the book take time. However, for some harmers they are at risk every day because of their self harming. Often it is important to take some steps straight away that are about keeping you safe and doing everything possible to reduce the risk of your coming to serious harm.

'Harm minimization' is mentioned as part of the NICE government guidelines for working with self harm. The central theme of harm minimization is that if self harm has to occur, it should be done in the way that causes the least damage, and good first aid practice has to be available afterwards.

There are practical things you can do to reduce the risk of self harm, whether you are the sufferer or someone caring for them. Many studies have shown that what people do can be influenced by what 'tools' are available. Lots of people react to this by trying to take away the things a sufferer uses to harm – confiscating blades or lighters to try to keep them safe. However, someone desperate to harm in order to feel better will find something to use, and taking away safer items may mean they resort to something more dangerous instead. So it is about making sure that these 'tools' are as safe as possible:

clean and sterile and not too sharp or large. If you or the person you are supporting has taken overdoses in the past, you might want to make sure that large quantities of drugs are not available. Think about how you can help practically – *not* by trying to take away the means of harming but by reducing the risk.

Once harming has occurred, the next important thing is to think about first aid. The aim here is obvious: clean the wound, close the wound and dress it well to prevent infection. If there is a need to seek medical help (for example, in cases of overdose), this should be done straight away. If you know you are at risk of needing medical help and might not go yourself, agree on a code word with a friend that you can call and say, or text, to them. They know that this means you have harmed and need help – you don't need to explain. Give yourself the best possible chance of staying healthy; you'll need to in order to have the chance to work on recovery.

Recovering from self harm is obviously about more than reducing harming. But this is an important step in the process. It's a step that people often miss out in their haste to change, but taking time at this stage will actually help you with recovery in the long term. So try not to get caught in feelings of despair or failure. The fact that you are thinking about reducing your self harming and are protecting yourself is a really important one. It's a great sign! Do what you can to reduce harming and keep yourself safe, and this will enable you to spend time focusing on some of the other issues that lie behind self harm.

For more advice on how to manage wounds so they heal well and have minimal scarring, see the Appendix at the end of this book.

8 Expressing emotion

In Chapter 3 we started to look at the way our emotions can build up, and how this can be linked with the desire to self harm. This chapter is all about how we can take that understanding and start to change the way we react to our emotions. If self harm is in part a strategy that some people use in order to deal with these painful emotions, then learning about emotions and how to handle them better is an essential stage of working to recovery.

So what exactly are emotions? Understanding this is really the first step in starting to deal with your emotions better. You need to know exactly what they are and what they are for. Emotions are not just random things that happen to affect us. In fact, they are a very important part of the way our brains work. Research was conducted by doctors working with a group of patients who had very unusual brain injuries that seemed to affect them by taking away their ability to experience normal emotions. These people said that they just didn't 'feel' things like sadness, anxiety and happiness any more. Now, some people would think that to be able to take emotion out of our minds would leave us much better able to think clearly and rationally. However, the truth is quite the opposite. People without emotions struggle with normal life: they find relationships and communication very difficult; they make bad decisions; they find making everyday choices very hard and often deliberate for hours over simple matters like what to have for breakfast. The loss of their emotions has a massive impact on how efficiently their brain works.

This is because emotions really do play an important role in your brain. There are lots of theories about exactly what they do, but emotions are basically like warning flags that alert us to the fact that something about what is going on in the world around us might be significant to us. Emotions move our attention to whatever this is, and give us the chance to analyse more in depth whether we need to react. Without them, we would be swamped with an overwhelming influx of information, and we wouldn't know what we needed to pay attention to.

So what exactly is an emotion? If we were to ask lots of people to think of the last time they experienced an emotion, and then describe what it was about the way they felt that made them label it as that emotion, they would usually include four different things in their descriptions (see Figure 2). First of all, they might talk about a *change in the way they were feeling physically*. Most emotions involve a physical or physiological change. So when we are anxious or angry our heart rate might go up, or when we are sad we might experience physical changes such as crying. The second thing people might mention is the way that *their thoughts change*. When we experience an emotion it triggers certain thoughts. So, anxiety makes us think about what is going to happen and worry about the unknown, and happiness fills our minds with positive thoughts. The third aspect often mentioned is the part of an emotional experience that *makes you want to do something*. Some emotions carry this more clearly than others. So, anger makes you want to lash out or do something physical. Other emotions make you want to withdraw and hide, or run and find people to share your joy. Emotions don't change our behaviour directly, but they give us an urge to behave in certain ways – making it more likely that we will do those things. Finally, the fourth characteristic of an emotion is much harder to label. It's an elusive quality that means that somehow *we just 'know'* we are having an emotion. Some emotions are much harder to describe than others. They are simply things we learn to label and experiences we become used to having.

Figure 2

'Other' feelings

Actions

EMOTION!

Thoughts

Physical feelings

From these four parts of an emotional experience, we can presume two main roles for emotions in our brains. First of all, emotions get our attention and help us to know which of the things that are going on around us need further thought or analysis. Second, emotions seem to have a role in preparing us for action, and they make us more likely to act in certain ways. For example, the phrase 'fight or flight' is often used to describe the way that emotions such as anger and anxiety prime the body to be ready to react if necessary. We also know that without emotions we are in trouble – they are not simply optional extras, but instead are a central part of the way the brain was designed to act.

This suggests that maybe we need to change the way we think about emotions. Many people think of them as a bit of a nuisance – something that they would really rather be without. Some of us have grown up in families in which certain emotions have not really been allowed, or in which we have been encouraged to hide our emotions rather than express them. Very often our reaction to an emotion that is inconvenient, painful, or one we think we maybe shouldn't be having, is to try to ignore or suppress it and hope it goes away. But emotions do not just go away. Suppressing an emotion is rather like dealing with a very angry cat by trying to put it in a box to get rid of it. You might manage to get it in there in the end and even shut the lid. But it is still there. You will hear it meow from time to time, and if it gets really mad a paw might stick out from under the lid. Keeping the lid on the box can become really exhausting – but, most important of all, I wouldn't want to be around when you finally let that cat out! By then the original emotion will have grown and merged with any others you had in that box, and will be really powerful and painful. It will be so detached from the original trigger that caused it that it will be very difficult to understand. It will feel out of control, nasty, and very strong. That is exactly what happens if people habitually suppress their emotions in an attempt to get rid of them: the box becomes a kind of bubbling pit of negative emotions. Remember that their role was to alert you to something, so they won't just go away. At some stage, often when you are feeling vulnerable – perhaps you are tired or on your own – those emotions will re-emerge (see Figure 3).

In order to start to handle our emotions better we need to remember what they are. Emotions are not choices – they are automatic responses triggered by our brains when we detect something going on that is significant. At this point it

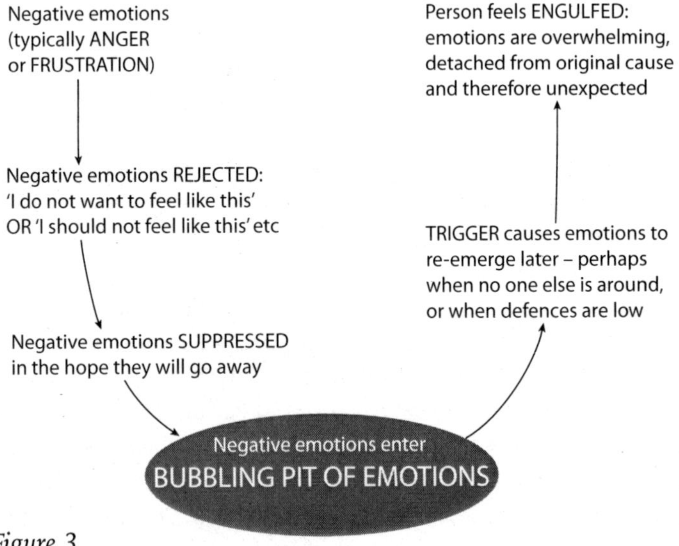

Negative emotions (typically ANGER or FRUSTRATION)

Person feels ENGULFED: emotions are overwhelming, detached from original cause and therefore unexpected

Negative emotions REJECTED: 'I do not want to feel like this' OR 'I should not feel like this' etc

TRIGGER causes emotions to re-emerge later – perhaps when no one else is around, or when defences are low

Negative emotions SUPPRESSED in the hope they will go away

Negative emotions enter
BUBBLING PIT OF EMOTIONS

Figure 3

is worth mentioning that often when emotions are causing problems, the root of them is that your brain is responding to situations which *used* to be significant long ago – perhaps when you were growing up. It may be that that response is now out of date – those situations just don't have the same meaning now that they used to – but your brain will still trigger the same emotion because it is warning you that years ago that combination of things happening probably led to an outcome that you would want to avoid. If you are having emotional reactions that you would rather not have, the way to deal with them is not to suppress them but to work out *why* your brain is triggering that emotion. What is it about the situation you were in that is, or used to be, significant? Only then can you start to work through the emotion and hopefully even get to a stage where those kinds of situations no longer trigger such a reaction. The other problem with suppressing emotions is that some people get so good at it that they do not even realize they are having emotional reactions. This means that they don't have the chance to deal with them one by one, and the only time they are aware of their emotions is when they become overwhelming. This makes emotions seem really scary, and leaves people feeling totally out of control of what they are feeling.

If you feel as though your emotions are out of control, don't despair. It *is* possible to be the one in control of your emotions. The first stage is really about becoming more aware of your emotions, and starting to pick up more acutely which ones you are experiencing and when. Imagine that your emotions are like little streams flowing towards the sea. Bit by bit those streams flow into a river so that the river grows. Each stream might be something quite minor, but they add up, and the river of emotion gets bigger and bigger. Eventually that river goes past a point of no return. It is flowing so big and fast that even if you wanted to turn round and do something to deal with those emotions you couldn't – they are just too strong.

It's at this point that lots of people start to feel the urge to harm. If you want to be able to deal with your emotions in a different way, you need to identify them before you get to that point of no return. You need to be able to start noticing the little streams as they join – or at least realize when the river is becoming big and powerful.

Quick tips on how to handle...

ANGER AND FRUSTRATION

Anger and frustration are often linked with self harm, because they carry with them such a strong urge to do something – often something destructive. Some people tend to turn that in on themselves. Anger is also a much more acceptable emotion to feel and express socially than some others (such as sadness, anxiety or jealousy), so sometimes anger is like a smokescreen covering up another emotion (that is, instead of allowing yourself to feel sad, anxious or jealous, you just get angry with yourself). Anger and frustration directed inwards can also stem from being very critical of yourself.

Anger is a very powerful emotion. Imagine feeling so worked up that you could explode, feeling your fists clenching by your side, and feeling it continue to build up until you can't seem to hold it in any longer. This is how a self harmer harming out of anger feels. Initially it can start with something small, but that self-hatred and frustration grows until it triggers the harming. Harming that results from anger can be done violently, and can be very serious. People may describe feeling as though they have lost control and then lashed out – and they may harm in more unusual ways, such as punching walls, breaking bones or cutting very deeply.

There are hundreds of detailed books and websites about anger management that look at alternative ways to express anger. The main thing is to find a way to get it turned out instead of in – and of course to do this in an acceptable or practical way. Try writing down all the things you are feeling, preferably using really angry colours, and then destroying the paper – maybe tearing it up into tiny pieces, burning it or shredding it. Some people find punching a punch bag or kicking something such as an old tyre helps. You may want to keep old plates or milk bottles to smash – although of course you need a safe place to do this, and enough patience to tidy up afterwards! Some sport can help you express anger – like squash, in which you can hit the ball as hard as you like. Or you can try shouting; find somewhere that no one can hear you and let rip, or shout into a pillow.

FEELING 'LOW', SAD OR DOWN
This set of difficult-to-describe emotions often occurs when you are overwhelmed emotionally in a vulnerable moment. When emotions that you have suppressed earlier in the day or week re-emerge, they are not specific and separate. Instead, you often end up dealing with a kind of soupy mixture of negative emotions, which can leave you feeling really flat, low and sorry for yourself. When you feel this low it may seem as if the only way you can express it is through harming.

If you can do only one thing when you are feeling like this, try to remember that things are not as bad as they seem. When you feel this low your brain plays tricks on you. You will find it harder than usual to solve problems, so you may feel that you have no options or that things are totally hopeless. You will also find yourself remembering all the other times you felt the same way – so it can seem in these moments as though you always feel this bad. This is not a good time to make any big decisions, so remember: it is an emotional fog and it will lift. Give it time.

The only way to respond to these sorts of emotion is to look after yourself. Think of how you would care for someone else who was feeling really low and miserable. Your body and brain are crying out to be looked after and cared for, so instead of slipping into negative thinking patterns, plan some activities that are 100 per cent designed to make you feel better. You may not feel like doing this because of the desire to punish yourself, but trust me – it is the best way to lift that mood and help yourself to feel better. Try doing something really self-indulgent: buy a magazine or a book, run a bath and chill! Other things that absorb your mind will be helpful, so try painting, embroidery (it may not be the coolest pastime but a lot of people find it really helpful, and you can watch TV whilst you do it!) or anything craft-related, such as making cards or candles. Some people find going to the cinema or watching films a good way to clear their minds (though be careful what kind of film you go to see – aim for a comedy or feel-good choice).

ANXIETY

Anxiety is one of the most common emotions to go unnoticed when it first starts. It's also a very common emotion to have trouble with, because if you do not find regular ways to relax, the baseline levels of the hormones and chemicals that regulate anxiety in your body will gradually rise. This means that even little things – things you would usually cope with – can make you feel overwhelmed. Anxiety often makes you feel as though you don't have any control, especially over the things that matter. Self harm can feel like a way of putting yourself back in control – but there are other, much more successful ways of dealing with anxiety and *really* getting back in control.

The way to deal with anxiety is to relax. As mentioned in Chapter 7, very few people build regular periods of relaxation into their day-to-day life, but everyone should do something relaxing for at least half an hour each day. So, to deal with anxiety, don't just wait for it to hit – build in regular time to chill out. A lot of people say that they just can't relax – and it is something you have to learn, so if you find it really hard then remember you will have to practise. As with anything else, try out as many different methods as you can and keep a note of which things you find helpful and which you do not. Ask your friends and family what they do to relax to get some ideas of things to try.

One thing you might want to try is to learn a specific relaxation method. A word of caution: relaxation classes are often something people find very hard at first. If you are really stressed out and tense, you might want to start with something else in order to get better at generally switching off and starting to relax. Otherwise, some people find that being put in a class and asked to relax is actually really stressful – so it has the opposite effect! Try getting hold of a CD or DVD that helps you learn to relax in an environment in which you feel comfortable, such as your bedroom or living room. Use other things that help you to relax and make sure you are warm, comfortable and feel safe. Don't forget that some other things can help, such as aromatherapy oils, candles and gentle lighting. Be creative and give yourself time to learn! (See Chapter 9 for more on relaxation.)

9 Negative thinking spirals

So far in this section of the book we've looked at some practical ideas of how to start working on recovery from self harm. We've also looked at the theory behind it, thinking about emotions and how they lead up to the urge to harm. But perhaps the biggest problem most sufferers find is that there are times when all this information seems irrelevant – when they feel so low and negative about themselves that any motivation goes, and self harm feels like the only option. As one sufferer said:

> 'The trouble is that I feel like two different people.
> When things are going ok I am able to think clearly,
> challenge things and handle my emotions pretty well.
> But in those moments when it really kicks off, someone
> else takes control of my head. It's like I am swamped
> with negative thoughts and there's nothing I can do to
> get out of that frame of mind. In those moments I try
> to remember all the stuff I believe about how I am not
> all bad, and how it isn't all hopeless, but it's really
> hard. It's like suddenly someone turns out the light and
> I just can't hold on to who I am any more.'

One of the key features of self harm is the negative thought cycles that people experience. They can seem to hit at any moment and are usually well rehearsed, word perfect and utterly powerful. They often represent all the worst fears that person has – things that they are constantly trying not to think. Then, at those low, vulnerable moments it's as if someone switches that thought stream back on. Negative thought cycles can go round and round in your head. They are hard to escape from and feel impossible to stop. They don't need to be based on fact because they feel so true – even if everyone else disagrees with them. Negative thought cycles can keep people feeling low for days at a time and in fact often bring people even lower. They can be like a downward spiral that leaves you feeling utterly desperate and hopeless.

It isn't just people who are self harmers who struggle against these kinds of unhelpful thought patterns. In fact, most people have moments when their thinking goes haywire and becomes unhelpful. But people who struggle with self harm – and other psychological problems such as addictions, eating disorders and depression – tend to experience these thoughts more regularly, and find them more powerful in terms of the emotions they trigger. They may find themselves caught up in negative spirals more often – and may find that self harm is part of their strategy to try to stop them and feel better.

We've talked in Chapters 3 and 8 about how emotions are a bit like automatic reflex reactions that are essential to the way the brain works. These kinds of emotions – short-term, appropriate (usually) and controllable – are what everyone encounters in day-to-day life. You simply can't avoid them. Imagine for a moment that you plotted your emotional life on a graph, scoring each day on a scale of -10 (feeling really low) to +10 (feeling utterly fantastic). You might plot a few points each day, and through doing this you could get an idea of roughly how you were feeling from week to week (see Figure 4). What do you think most people's graphs would look like?

The answer is that most people – those who are not struggling with any emotional problems – find that on average their days are somewhere in the range of about

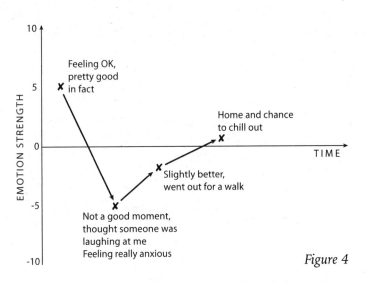

Figure 4

-1 or -2 to 5. That is, on the whole they feel positive, not wildly so, but definitely positive, with occasional blips in which they drop into a negative mood. Interestingly, most people will talk about what they do and how they react if they find themselves falling below that baseline – perhaps phoning a friend to have a good moan, planning a chilled out evening to cheer themselves up or trying to do something about whatever caused them to feel low in the first place. Of course, every once in a while life throws something at you that triggers a real high or a real low. But, on the whole, those times are infrequent and unusual.

I wonder whether this surprises you at all. Sometimes people who are struggling with their emotions get the impression that everyone else enjoys a blissfully happy existence, floating along in the +5 to +10 region all the time. This can make you feel even worse if you are having a bad week yourself, and it's important to be aware of what 'normal' really is – and make sure you are not putting too much pressure on yourself. If you plotted your emotions on a graph, what would you find? One thing that people with depression, or who self harm, or who have similar problems often talk about is how hard they find it the minute they start to fall into that negative zone. Remember, sparks of emotion (positive and negative) are normal – and even important. So it is not unusual or unexpected to occasionally fall below zero. But how you react to being there is very important. Some studies discuss the concept of emotion tolerance – which really is talking about how well people cope with experiencing negative emotions such as anxiety. Some people seem to be so panicked by the experience of having a negative emotion spark that it triggers these negative thinking patterns, which, in turn, make the emotions worse.

Think of it like this: the everyday emotions we all experience are like striking a match – they spark, flame and die out pretty quickly. They do what they are supposed to do and then they resolve. But for a lot of people, their patterns of negative thinking and other things, such as experiences they have had in the past, beliefs they hold about who they are or are not, and things people have said to them over the years – all these things are like kindling, like dry leaves on the floor of a forest in a hot summer. They lie there waiting for a spark, and when one comes, instead of burning small and briefly, it builds up very quickly into an enormous fire – fuelled by all those thoughts, beliefs and memories. So one emotional spark can then lead to an enormous blaze of emotion and thoughts that can be really difficult to deal with (see Figure 5).

Emotion sparks happen to all of us, every day, and are the way emotions are designed to work. They are short-lived, manageable and help us to focus on a potential problem, analyse it and decide whether any action is required. However, if those sparks trigger unhelpful thinking patterns, they can cause the emotion to grow and become very powerful, setting off secondary emotional reactions as

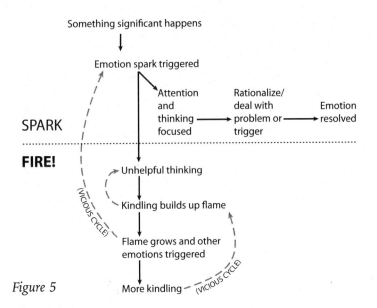

Figure 5

well. These vicious cycles carry on and on, so that we can become overwhelmed with very powerful emotions – like a fire burning out of control. We cannot stop ourselves from experiencing emotion sparks – the top part of this diagram is automatic and an important part of how our brain works. But the bottom half – where fires develop – can be under our control. So it is possible to learn to control your emotions and stop them burning so fiercely.

Six unhelpful thought patterns
So what kinds of thoughts make up this kindling and leave us so prone to having trouble with our emotions? There are basically six main types of thoughts that have been linked to having emotional problems. The first two are common in anyone who is a classic pessimist. They are about *looking at the world through a negative filter* so that you only take notice of negative things – and about only *predicting negative things for the future*. You'll find this kind of thought pattern

in people who are very self-critical. They will look back on their day and recall only the negative things – things they did wrong or things that didn't go well. They could have a 99 per cent good day but spend their evening dwelling on the 1 per cent that was not so great. Then they will often also make negative predictions. They assume that if anything can go wrong it probably will, and often spend a lot of time worrying about things that in fact never happen. Both of these thinking styles are often closely linked with a tendency to be perfectionistic, as is the next one: *all or nothing thinking*. All or nothing thinking is about treating the world as if it is in black and white, with no shades of grey in between: you either succeed or you fail. People who think like this often put a tremendous amount of pressure on themselves, aiming to be pretty much perfect in all they do and really feeling bad if they 'fail'. Thinking in this way is often linked with having a real fear of failure, which is why it triggers so much negative emotion – because this pattern of thinking leaves you feeling as though you fail all the time. After all, how often do you have a 100 per cent perfect day? All or nothing thinking also makes working on recovery hard, because people who think like this tend to set themselves unrealistic goals, and then really struggle if they do not achieve them. The normal ups and downs of recovery can then be really difficult to handle, and leave them at risk of slipping into a negative spiral.

All or nothing thinking is quite closely linked to the pattern of thinking called *catastrophizing* or *snowballing*. This is when someone (often a person who wanted everything to go perfectly) focuses on small negative things that have happened and treats them as indicators that everything is going to be a disaster from that point on. So, for example, burning the toast one morning can make you feel as if the entire day is going to be a nightmare – no one will listen to what you have to say, no one will turn up to the evening do you have planned, and you will end up with no friends and be alone forever. Writing down the trains of thought can make them seem almost comical, but at the time you really do feel as bad as the last thought: you feel that you will be alone forever. It's only when you analyse your thinking that you realize that all this actually stems from... burning the toast. Your thinking has taken anxious leaps along a pathway of your worst fears when in fact those links are not logical and don't really follow on.

Negative mind-reading is the fifth common unhelpful thinking style. This is when you *think* you know what people are thinking, but the funny thing is that people who do this will only ever 'read' thoughts in other people's minds about themselves that are negative. Very rarely do they think that someone is impressed with how funny they are, or that someone really likes their new hairstyle. No, instead they worry that those people are laughing at them, that everyone thinks they are stupid, that no one takes them seriously. Negative mind-reading is nasty because those things are never put into words, so you never get the chance to test them. As a result, people often assume their thoughts are right – and this leaves them feeling very self-conscious and anxious. Negative mind-reading often results in people avoiding company when they are feeling low – which makes them feel much worse and leads to the isolation that can make those negative spirals even worse.

The last common negative thought pattern is to do with *magnifying negatives and minimizing positives*. A lot of people do this, and it's quite similar to looking at the world through a negative filter. This is about ignoring any successes you have had and playing them down ('Anybody could have done it... It wasn't that hard really... Actually, I was just really lucky... I think the examiner took pity on me'), and at the same time coming down on yourself really hard if you ever do things wrong ('I am so stupid – why am I always stupid?... This is just typical of me... Everyone else got it right, I was the only one to fail'). It's not hard to see how this kind of pattern can contribute to a negative spiral in which you end up feeling as if everything you do goes wrong, and that you are utterly useless.

We all slip into these thinking styles from time to time. The problem is when you find that they dominate your thinking regularly, so that they build up that layer of emotional 'kindling'. Then, when you have a negative emotion spark, it builds straight into a fire. Ultimately, these thinking errors are so powerful because we tend to make a basic mistake: we believe that our thoughts and beliefs *must* be truth – that is, because I think this, it must be true. We can do the same with emotions, thinking, for example, that because we feel guilty, we *must be* guilty. This simply isn't the case. Thoughts and beliefs come from lots of different places and are not always totally reliable, particularly if they occur whilst we are in the middle of powerful emotions. This is doubly true if you had a difficult start in life, because a lot of our thought patterns and beliefs are formed in childhood. So it may be that the things you have always believed to be true simply aren't – but they might be having a huge impact on the way you think and feel.

The other reason negative thinking spirals are so powerful is because they lead people to feel trapped in their own thoughts. Thoughts that are negative and powerful are very hard to share, and you may feel that no one understands you. This contributes to feelings of isolation and can mean that people avoid social situations and withdraw from friendships and relationships that would actually help and support them. Loneliness and isolation are two of the most common issues described by those who suffer with self harm. Self harmers often struggle with forming close friendships, perhaps finding it hard to trust or fearing that people will not like them. They also often find it hard or impossible to communicate their emotions to their friends, therefore finding that, whilst in the happy times they have people around them, it is very hard to access support when they are struggling with negative feelings. Many feel as though they live double lives, covering up the negative thoughts and fears they have about themselves and never understanding why anyone would want to be their friend. Being genuinely alone is bad enough, but the actual presence of other people doesn't guarantee that loneliness will be banished. It is common for sufferers to report feeling dreadfully lonely even when in busy places, particularly in social situations in which others are chatting and circulating such as parties, coffee mornings, churches and other social gatherings. The tendency to feel like this is linked to issues such as low self-esteem, anxiety and difficult relationships or the absence of friendships early in life. It is also one of the reasons that self harm is more likely in those who are divorced, live alone or are single parents. Ultimately, the first step in forming good friendships and relationships is to believe you have something to offer – and negative thinking spirals challenge this most basic of beliefs.

The first step in overcoming negative thinking patterns is to be aware that they exist. Do you find that as soon as you slip into feeling negative, things just spiral and grow? Are you afraid of feeling anything negative because it has so often led to long-lasting times of feeling down? If so, chances are that these negative patterns are behind it. Treating these thinking patterns, identifying them and ultimately starting to challenge them is the basis of cognitive behavioural therapy (CBT), which is the treatment most recommended not just for self harm but for all kinds of psychological and emotional problems. Changing your thinking is not easy, and it takes time, great support and a lot of energy. But it is possible. Try to change the way you think about your emotions: instead of being scared of the negative sparks, be analytical about them. What kinds of things trigger them? Do you find that there are particular thoughts, worries or beliefs that you really struggle with when you are feeling low? Are they things that your friends and family would disagree with, but that feel powerfully true to you at the time?

Ultimately this is what makes negative thoughts so powerful – the fact that when you 'hear' them, you believe that they are true. There are two types of information in the world. Some things are just facts: they are objective and true and we cannot argue with them – such as how long something is, or how much it weighs. Other kinds of information are quite different, however: they are opinion, not fact, and some people may agree whilst others disagree. If I think a colour is nice or that something tastes good, these are not solid facts, they are my opinions. Negative thoughts become a problem when we take the second kind of information – an opinion – and treat it like a fact. So if you think 'I can't believe I did that wrong, I am really stupid', that is an opinion, not a fact – which is why someone else may well disagree, and perhaps tell you that you were being too harsh on yourself. But people who struggle with their thoughts believe them as though they were facts, and that makes them very powerful.

So understanding your thought spirals won't make them go away, but you will be surprised how it does help you to feel less out of control. Just making that little step from thinking 'I am stupid' to thinking 'I feel like I am stupid', just realizing that those thoughts are opinions and not facts, is the first step to being able to change the way you think. Perhaps most of all, though, if you take one thing from this chapter, remember that your thinking is not always reliable. Just because you think it, doesn't mean it is true!

10 Coming to terms with scarring

One of the most difficult things that someone who self harms faces in the long term is how to deal with the scars on their body. For many people scarring is a permanent effect of self harm, and for some, scars become a lifetime reminder of their struggle. Scars can raise questions in others, cause anxiety for sufferers, create challenges to people's self-confidence and, for some, even make them feel that they cannot move on. Scars are an indicator of things we have been through – illnesses, operations and injuries. The problem with scars is that they persist long after the illness that caused them has been resolved. The other main issue with scarring is that the presence of scarring can in effect disclose to someone else that you have a history of self harm. Whereas most people who have recovered from a psychological illness have a choice about when and who they tell, scars may take that control away.

This chapter will look at how to start to come to terms with scars. However, some people will want to know about the practical issues involved with scarring, including scar reduction (how to try to avoid getting too many obvious scars in the first place) and methods to minimize or disguise scars. For this, please refer to the Appendix at the end of the book, 'Minimizing and disguising scars'.

People deal with the marks of their self harm in many ways. Some people insist on wearing long sleeves and woolly jumpers all the time – even through the heat of summer. They prefer questions about why they are dressed for winter to questions about self harm. It seems to be much easier to deal with questions regarding something they have chosen, rather than something that is associated with shame and isolation. This does, however, lead to a life of distracting others from the scars in the hope of not having to deal with their shock or judgement, and it brings with it some obvious problems.

Some self harmers, as part of their process of recovery, find themselves feeling very angry about people's reactions. These feelings may become tangled up with other anger and frustration, and leave them feeling that they want to have the right to display their scars. Some will deliberately dress to reveal the scars, making it clear they have self harmed and demanding a reaction. This way of dealing with the issue is just as understandable as trying to cover up the scars, but it can make people feel very uncomfortable and evoke reactions that may not be constructive.

Of course, some sufferers, genuinely having moved on, simply wear clothes that they like – just like anyone else. However, the issue of how to handle responses and reactions to scars is something that almost all recovered sufferers will have to deal with. After all, dealing with scars is not just about how you feel. In fact, often a decision over how to handle the issue of scarring is as much related to other people's reactions as it is to your own. Most recovered harmers will need to accept that questions will be asked at some stage. Take the experience of one recovered sufferer, who had prolifically self harmed over a number of years and was one day wearing a vest top, as it was a hot summer day. She went to buy some cigarettes and, as anybody would do, she looked the sales woman in the eye and asked for her particular brand. The lady, a complete stranger, responded with pursed lips, saying angrily, 'That's such a waste of time; it won't get you any sympathy from me.' This kind of reaction is difficult to handle and can trigger the very emotions that sufferers are working desperately hard to learn how to deal with. As a result, the stage of starting to be more open with scarring can be a significant challenge along the road to recovery. Another recovered sufferer, applying for a job as a youth worker, was asked extensively in an interview how she would handle explaining the cause of her scars to the young people she worked with. This question, although uncomfortable for her, was an issue she really did need to think about because the questions and interest her scars would trigger from the young people she planned to care for needed careful answering. These kinds of issues – whether representing acceptable and justifiable questioning or originating from misunderstanding and misconceptions – are what many self harmers contend with every day.

Dealing with your own reaction to scarring

The process of deciding how to deal with scars is one that takes time. A lot of sufferers find that they adopt different approaches at different stages of their recovery. On the whole, dealing with other people's responses is something that comes after dealing with your own issues and emotions, and you may find it easier to cover up scars at first – although you may be able to be more relaxed with close family and friends who know about your self harm. However, there is likely to come a stage when you feel more able to start to accept those scars as part of yourself – and can then move on to other ways of dealing with them. The ultimate goal is about becoming comfortable with who you are: accepting all that made you the person you are, including a period of time in your life when self harm was an issue. Dealing with scars, and the shame that may go with them, often forms part of this process of acceptance.

The reality is that our bodies are marked in so many ways by our lifestyle choices, our habits and what we do with our time. Diet, exercise, smoking, drinking, piercings, tattoos... the list goes on. Our bodies tend to hold the markers and signs of the things that we have been through and experienced in our lives. Like it or not, this is unavoidable. Scars remind us of what has happened – sometimes of specific traumatic memories – and often coming to terms with scars is as much about working through and accepting past events as it is about dealing with the scars themselves. We all have a plan in our minds when we are young of what we think our life will look like. Usually it's a pretty rosy plan that fits in with what we see as the 'norms': we plan to be happy, successful, get married, have kids... Lots of people, however, hit a stage in their lives when they have to accept that things did not go according to plan. Self harm certainly falls into that category. Very few people planned as children to spend any part of their life struggling with feeling so low and sad. But the risk is that you spend so long fighting with yourself – not wanting to accept that self harm is something that has happened in your life – that, as a result, you find it very hard to move on. Scars can then be really difficult because they remind you of something that you do not want to accept has really happened. But having self harm in your life story does not need to ruin it. Many people have struggled with issues in their lives, and most 'normal' people have some difficult periods. In fact, having life fit in with the naïve plans that we make when we're young is really rare! Remember, success is not about avoiding slipping up; it is much more about what you *do* once you have slipped up. The key to starting to handle issues around scarring is to allow yourself to accept what you have been through. It is about finding a way to make self harm a part of your life story, without it ending up as the main theme. The whole story of who you are doesn't end with self harm; it includes your working through it as one chapter. Once you can start to see it like this you can look to end that chapter and move on to the next one – and it is at this point that dealing with scars may start to get easier.

Other people's reactions
It's a simple fact that for a lot of sufferers the worst thing about scars is not how they make them feel, but worrying about how other people will react to them. Be aware that this worrying is often much worse than the reality of the actual reactions! Many recovered sufferers spend years worrying about what it will be like when people notice their scars, but when they finally take the step of dressing in what they want rather than in what their scars dictate, they find that many people don't notice, don't comment, or are not too bothered by what they see. In fact, as awareness and understanding of self harm increases, this is likely to improve. What this might help you start to realize is that what seemed huge to you just wasn't as enormous as you thought. In fact, a lot of fears are like that. We worry about the worst-case scenario, but if it ever does happen it's often nothing like as bad as the experience of worrying about it beforehand! What this shows is the power that self harm can have over you – even when it is not something you do any more – and the limitations that it can place on you. Ultimately, recovery is about finding a freedom from these fears as well as from the self harm itself.

If someone does respond negatively to your scarring, then the first thing to do is to distance yourself from that person. Try not to react straight away because you need to give yourself time to rationalize what you have just heard with what you know to be true. Remember, sometimes we let comments get to us that were made by people who know nothing about self harm or about us! Don't place too much weight on an opinion that comes from such ignorance, and don't let it get under your skin and start to bother you. Be particularly careful of these kinds of comments setting off one of the negative spirals we talked about in Chapter 9. You know the kind of thing: 'They're right – I am mad. I always knew it... I guess I'll always be a failure... I might as well not bother...' Hold on to the truths you know, and try not to slip into believing the thoughts triggered by feelings that thoughtless comments sparked.

If the comment came from someone you don't know and won't see again, then sometimes you simply have to let it go. We all receive comments sometimes that are unjust, and, on the whole, the battle just isn't worth fighting. However, if it is someone you know, or someone you come across regularly (maybe a relative or colleague), or if it is someone who you think just *should* know better about how to respond, you might want to think about how to help them gain a better understanding of self harm. Perhaps you could leave a copy of a book like this one in a strategic place for them! Remember first and foremost, though, that your priority is self-protection. Only tackle them if you can cope with their reaction. If you are at a vulnerable place in your recovery or are having a bad week/month/year, it's ok to just put it behind you and leave well alone.

Real-life experiences…
What made you decide to start working on recovery?

NINA

'I think the main thing that made me want to stop cutting was fear of the actual harm I might do myself. I started by being afraid of infection, but somewhat bizarrely I tried burning myself instead. Burning was also a bit easier to do on a less-planned and thought-through basis, and so I guess I could kid myself that it had just sort of happened. I also didn't have to worry about where the burns were because anyone who saw would just assume it was an accident.

'Actually, in terms of being afraid of infection, it was a bad move and I didn't actually do it too many times – the burns were worse than the cuts because a couple of times I accidentally burnt deeper than I'd meant and had to go to the chemist to check that they weren't infected 'cos they were looking decidedly yucky. That made me want to stop because my far too vivid imagination would imagine it getting infected and having to have my arm amputated! The burns also gave me a reason to look after myself – I could see they needed looking after and protecting to heal – the kind of treatment I wasn't giving myself as a whole.

'There wasn't only the fear of doing real harm; there were a lot of other negative sides to the self harm. Partly the loneliness that I've already mentioned – that the sense in which it gave me control, and a sense in which it wrapped a protective cocoon around me which no one else could get inside because it was my secret, was actually outweighed by the resulting loneliness. There were the massive feelings of guilt and failure. I'm quite an open person with the people that are close to me, and the self harm made me feel as if the people close to me didn't know me properly because there was a bit of myself I couldn't share with them.

'Then there was the inconvenience. Even though I was only cutting up the top of my arms so no one had to see, there were weddings when I'd have to do cover-up jobs with make-up. Sometimes the fear of people finding out stopped me doing it. I love swimming in the sea, and knowing I wanted to do that in the summer stopped me for a couple of months beforehand.'

JIM

'I remember it was one night after cutting myself that I decided I needed help. I jumped down from my bed and walked into my mum's room. To my memory I was covered in blood, and I handed her a razor blade and told her I needed help. She was unbelievable. She never judged me. From so many accounts from other people I have met, and their stories of when their parents found out, I am truly blessed. Mum was of course confused, hurt, worried, anxious – but calm and clever. She found out everything she could about self harm. She removed all rough and rusty blades from my room and left only clean razor blades – she had watched a programme that said I would find a way to cut myself, and it would be better with a clean, sharp knife than a rough, unhygienic one. Mum also prayed for me. Over and over. Sometimes I would go to her when the darkness came over me and she would calm me. Other times I would retreat into myself and not tell her what was going on.

'My A levels began to be hell. I was clever, but with my shattered mind, with the whiskey, with the lack of sleep, it all fell apart. Still no one knew. My teachers began to talk to me about dropping their courses. I was failing every mock test. I begged to be allowed to stay on their courses. I think they allowed me to just to help me not fall apart. I also told two friends. One understood – the other didn't understand but allowed me to be myself. I then told another friend, and she told me I was selfish and that I should be ashamed of myself. I was and didn't tell anyone else after that.

'I finished A levels and managed to do very well, but mentally

I was a total mess. I moved straight away to Coventry to attend Bible college. That was a very hard time. I was alone and struggled with my studies. I felt very low, and did my best not to cut myself – but I couldn't stop. No one knew what was going on. Eventually I started getting counselling to help me talk through my life and the pain.'

RACHAEL

'There were lots of negatives to self harm which made me want to stop. One of the biggest disadvantages was the effect my behaviour had on my husband and close family. It left my husband extremely distressed and worried. It affected all my relationships in a negative way, often leaving me very alone and isolated because other people would no longer help me when I had self harmed in any way. I would have to get myself to hospital on my own. My friends no longer called me by phone when they heard I had been in hospital. Often friends did not know what to say to me. My husband stuck by me through all the experiences because he was very loyal and loved me, but I think had my self harm continued at the rate it was, then my marriage could have been at risk.

'I found that my injuries got progressively worse and that I took more risks when it came to overdosing to produce the desired effects. Scarring was also a big problem to me, as I developed scars which will never go completely, though I can use camouflage make-up to cover them up on special occasions. Day to day if I wear short sleeves I get asked questions and people treat me differently because of my scars. Overdosing brought with it many problems. I would often find myself in hospital and would behave in a violent manner towards staff and my family and would be disorientated and confused. After I left hospital I would have to explain what happened to family and friends, which would often cause much upset and distress.

'Things started to change when I started seeing a new psychologist under the NHS. We agreed a contract where, if I asked for help before self harming, I could see my psychologist often on the same day or when he was available, but if I self harmed, I was not allowed to see him for a week. It took a while for me to find this helpful, but gradually I learned to ask for help before I acted on my thoughts or feelings.

'At first, trying to stop self harming was about distracting myself and finding activities that I enjoyed doing rather than self harming. It took a while to build up a good relationship with my psychologist, but over time I started to learn a new way of communicating my needs verbally rather than harming. One of the big lessons I had to learn was to cope with my feelings without overdosing or self harming. I gradually learnt to rely on people and communicate with them rather than dealing with things myself in a destructive manner.'

LIBBY

'The point I got to when I felt I had to stop was around the time of my eighteenth. It all came to a head with my family and my boyfriend, and they joined forces to tell me how they felt about it. I realized that I either had to stop doing what I was doing or risk losing both of them. Around this time there was also once when I had cut quite deep and needed medical attention. I called my boyfriend to ask him to take me to hospital and he said no. He said it to help – if he had come running I may have used him – but at the time I was stunned that he could leave me like that. I felt too ashamed to tell my parents about it as they had company over, and to walk downstairs and ask them to take me to hospital would have embarrassed them far too much. This was such a low point because I knew that I needed help, but no one wanted to be there.

'For me therapy didn't help at all. When I finally managed to get the courage to go to the doctor and explain how I felt and that I thought I was depressed, it was chucked back in my face and I was told that I was just attention-seeking. I thought that must be true and I felt really stupid about it. Then, after I took *the overdose, I was pushed up the list to see a psychotherapist, but for me this didn't help either because there was no routine to it. But what did help was that they told me that I was depressed, slightly bipolar and struggling with self-destructive behaviour. Knowing that there was something wrong with me and putting a label on it helped a lot because it made sense of the way I felt.'*

Part 3

For those caring for sufferers

11 On discovering self harm – first reactions

Part 3 of this book is written for those who are involved with supporting sufferers – perhaps as part of their job or because friends or family members are struggling with self harm. How we handle self harm is the key to looking after ourselves as we support others and in supporting the harmer themselves. This chapter looks at the issues triggered when you first find out that someone is harming. From considering how people often react when they encounter self harm through to what action needs to be taken, it will offer advice for what to do when you are in the early stages of supporting someone.

When you have just found out...
One of the most important things when you find out that someone is self harming is how you react to that discovery in the first place. What you do and how you react will often determine how the harmer feels about sharing things with you in the future. It's important to realize just how much thought, planning and plucking up of courage might have gone into telling you. Issues such as whom to tell and how or when to try to explain – these are not things that sufferers take lightly. On the whole, self harm is not disclosed by accident, even though it may seem this way. It may look to you as if you discovered it by accident, but often this represents someone who actually did want someone (you) to find out. Some sufferers really struggle with whether or not to tell anyone, perhaps just not knowing how to go about it or worrying about whether it is the right thing

to do. Some, therefore, end up taking bigger and bigger 'risks' with actions that might lead to someone finding out (for example, not covering scars as well as usual or leaving diaries out). It's as though if someone finds out, this stops them from having to make the decision to tell.

It may be, however, that the person you are caring for chose to tell you directly about their self harm – either face to face or by email or letter. This is a hugely brave step, and it is important that you understand just how much courage it will have taken them to do this – and the risk that they have taken. They cannot control your reaction – but it really is crucial. In a way, through your reaction they can get a view of their self harm from a different perspective – a more distant one than the viewpoint they usually have. If you react well, then this will help them deal with the self harm themselves in a more positive way – and it will help them to overcome the very self-critical attitude that most sufferers tend to adopt.

If someone ever does disclose to you – whether by apparent 'accident' or deliberately – that they are self harming or have self harmed, it means that they see you as someone who may be able to help, someone they trust or someone they feel very close to and don't want to keep secrets from. Either way, it is a huge compliment and privilege. If they haven't chosen to disclose but you have found out, the privilege is no less, and how you respond is even more important because of the risk that they might panic, feel out of control of the situation, or wish that they could turn back time and stop you from finding out! One small encouragement, though, is that research suggests that your response is unlikely to affect the amount an individual is self harming, other than perhaps a minor blip at the point of disclosure.

Do...

What sufferers want when they have just admitted to their self harm is acceptance, unconditional love and recognition that they are not defined by the self harm (that they are still a person with value who has good points and bad points; they are more than just 'a self harmer'). Remember that this is true – that person is someone who is struggling with self harm. It need not define them or their future. So, if you are in any doubt, show them how you care about them, and worry about what you are going to do to support them more long term later. The more approachable and non-judgemental you can be, the better the chance that they will be able to come to you with the ups and downs of working on recovery. This won't in itself reduce the self harm, but it gives them a huge advantage because they won't be going it alone.

Try not to...

Reactions to try to avoid are those that leave the individual feeling judged and isolated. These risk pushing the harming behaviour underground and back into secrecy, as well as adding to feelings of shame, guilt and self-hatred. What you have at the time of disclosure is a window of opportunity in which the harmer has the chance to think about how they feel about self harming. You become like a mirror in which they can see a reaction to their own self harming. If that reaction is to put them down or reject them, this just adds to the thought patterns and feelings that actually keep the self harm going. You may think that you can 'shock them out of it' or that, by being nice, you are just encouraging the behaviour – but this simply isn't the case. Remember, self harm is a coping strategy – the only way they know how to deal with negative emotions and difficult feelings. If your reaction produces more of those feelings, the likelihood is that it will make things worse, not better. The only route to real recovery is for them to get help, work through those emotions and learn better ways of coping.

A word about disgust

Disgust is a very powerful emotion. Studies looking at emotions show how strong disgust – and the reactions it provokes – can be, and how difficult it is not to react when certain things are around (things that are likely to be unclean, infectious or that may make you ill produce the strongest reactions). Some people have a disgust reaction to anything involving wounds or blood – they would say that they are very squeamish. If this is you, you are likely to find it really difficult to deal with wounds. Do not ever try to hide disgust – it's really hard to cover it up, and the likelihood is that the sufferer will notice. If you don't talk about how you are feeling, they will take the emotion upon themselves. So, instead of the reality, 'They are disgusted by that wound', they will be thinking, 'They are disgusted with me.' The latter is a much more painful, personal attack on themselves, so it is really important you admit to what you are feeling and make sure you are clear that it is the wound you find hard, not the person. On the whole, it is best to make your reference to this as brief as possible – don't dwell on it, perhaps just briefly say that you are no good with anything medical and then move on.

Some sufferers themselves will struggle with feelings of disgust. These may be linked to wounds and to what they have done to themselves, and often it will be hard for them not to translate those feelings to being disgusted with themselves. You can help them to avoid that – make clear to them the difference between an emotional reaction to the wound and an emotional reaction to them. They need to know you love and care for them and that their wounds do not change that.

What to do if you blew it

It may well be that a lot of people reading this will have already had that moment when they first found out that someone was self harming. In fact, that may be why you went out and bought the book! If you are reading this thinking, 'That's all very well but it's too late now!', don't panic. If you didn't react well in that first moment, it is not the end of the world and you may be able to rectify the situation by what you do now.

First of all, don't be too hard on yourself. It can be a dreadful shock to discover self harm, and, for a lot of adults, especially parents, it is something that simply didn't happen 'in your day'. That makes it a totally new phenomenon, and one that is very frightening to deal with. Self harm triggers a lot of complex emotions, and you cannot avoid or deny those feelings – particularly if you had no warning or did not expect what you found out. Be honest with yourself and don't beat yourself up over what are often automatic reactions. You need to work through those feelings and work with the person you are supporting as well.

If your initial reaction to the self harmer was negative, the situation can be redeemed, but it will require long periods of offering affirming and positive responses. You will have to be prepared to be totally honest and to make yourself very vulnerable to that person. Remember, supporting that person does not mean that you have to support self harming. However, recovery does not happen overnight, and an attitude that asks them to stop immediately simply won't be helpful and is more likely to cause other problems. Remember that you don't have to treat the self harm yourself. Don't take too much on! You are not expected to be an expert on self harm. Your job is to be there to support the person you love as they seek treatment and to keep on giving them the tools they need to get well: acceptance, love and support.

Sometimes things go so badly the first time someone discloses their self harm that it is very difficult to open communication at all afterwards. Parents in particular risk being shouted out of the room or meeting complete silence and a refusal to speak. Just remember that the person who may be behaving in a pretty horrible way is actually terrified, desperate and very frightened. You need to find a way to communicate with them in which they can feel safe and back in control. A lot of people find leaving notes or even sending an email a good way to get back in touch. Do it in a very non-threatening way: put a note somewhere where they will see it. In the note explain that you did not handle things well when you spoke to them. Don't be afraid to admit that you were wrong. Promise not to mention it face to face again unless they want to talk, but explain that you love them and want to help. Offer them the chance to write back to you. This may seem like a theatrical way to get things moving but it may just take the heat out of the situation and get you talking again.

Overall, remember that your first reaction to finding out about someone's struggle with self harm is just that: it's a first reaction. Whatever you did or didn't do right or wrong, there is always time to change that. Recovery from self harm is a journey, not an instant change, and your support will mean everything to the person you are helping along the way.

Two common mistakes in caring for sufferers
A lot of caring comes from instinct. This is natural, no matter how much reading up and learning about self harm you do. That is why it is important to know the two main ways in which your instinct may tell you to do something that actually will not be helpful!

WANTING TO TAKE CONTROL

When they discover what is going on, a lot of people find themselves overwhelmed with a desire to take control over the sufferer's life. This is an understandable instinctive reaction for a problem in which someone seems so totally out of control. Where self harm is concerned, it usually leads people to do something to try to stop the harm – perhaps offering to take the sufferer's blades away, removing all the tools they can use to harm or keeping them supervised at all times to make sure they are safe. Discovering the self harm has triggered a fear reaction, and taking control feels as though it will reduce that fear and keep the sufferer safe.

The trouble is that taking away the sufferer's tools generally doesn't do either of these things. Recovering from self harm requires working through the thought patterns and emotions that lie behind it. Sheer will and determination not to harm will only last so long and risks emotions building up until they become so powerful that they cannot be ignored. Self harmers can be very creative when they need to be, and, on the whole, if somebody needs to harm, they will. Removing their normal routine often only adds to the crisis of the situation, making them feel trapped. It can even make the harming more serious as they seek out new ways to do it (see Chapter 7, page 68–69). Countless sufferers have described how, having given away their razors, lighters or whatever they usually used to harm, they ended up doing more damage as they frantically tried to find another way to deal with the emotional pain they were in. Once self harm has escalated (got more serious), it tends to stay at that higher level. So taking away 'safer' tools may have a long-term negative impact and actually make recovery harder.

The other risk is that if you try to stop them harming, then the self harm may also go on in secret. And, whatever else is true, self harm is better out in the open: it keeps sufferers safer and reduces the risk of it escalating. Remember, what you want is to help them get back in control, not to end up in the driving seat yourself.

TRYING TO GO TOO FAST

The second most common mistake people make in trying to help sufferers is to set goals that are too high, and to do this without them being that person's own choice. Again, this is understandable, especially when you are faced with someone who so desperately wants to get better. It is very hard to understand the emotional patterns and the strength of the emotional pain that go on behind self harm. Remember, sufferers have spent years learning how to use self harm to cope with emotions. Don't expect them to learn an alternative in a matter of weeks. Many sufferers are desperately keen to stop harming and wish that they did not have to do it. The feelings that people experience that lead them to harm are so painful and awful that they would give anything to be able not to have to experience them. They may genuinely want to hear that they can recover in a very short time. Much as you wish that this was true and you could make them better soon, all you will do is create unrealistic expectations.

Bear in mind in those moments when things are hard for them, when emotions feel overwhelming, how hard it is not to do the one thing they have found that helps those feelings go away. That is why stopping self harming is a step-by-step process. The risk of pushing a sufferer to stop too soon or of placing unhelpful expectations on them is that you will add to the weight of emotions, and also cause them to worry that they are letting you down. This will not help them to recover and may even make their self harm worse. Instead, help them to work through what they are feeling and encourage them to form positive goals. Rather than focusing on not harming, aim for doing something positive to deal with those emotions, perhaps working through a list of other things they can try to do to change how they are feeling (see Chapter 6, page 59–60). Support every little step forward, and reassure them when they seem to take a step backwards. This is a normal part of recovery.

12 Some additional thoughts for parents

'It was a horrible, terrible shock. I knew that she was having some problems at school and was a bit down. I'd even reconciled myself to the fact that she was probably a bit depressed and I was thinking of taking her to the doctor's. But finding out about the self harm was a total shock. I just didn't know what to do. All my instincts as a mum to keep that utterly precious child safe – and yet she was harming herself. I don't think anything could have prepared me for it.'

SALLY, WHO FOUND OUT THAT HER FOURTEEN-YEAR-OLD DAUGHTER JO WAS SELF HARMING REGULARLY

Supporting people who self harm is always challenging. However, most youth leaders and other professionals have, to some degree, chosen to do so and should have some knowledge and/or support themselves. However, for parents this isn't the case, and for many, the first time they have ever thought much about self harm is when they find out that it is affecting their child. If you are in that position, this chapter is for you.

Most parents go through a whole gamut of feelings at disclosure. These may include: panic ('Will my child die? Are they trying to kill themselves?'); blame ('It must be because I did something wrong. Is it because I never did so and so?'); guilt ('I've failed to be what I should be'); and shame ('What will others think of me?'). Many just want to keep it all secret – especially from their friends or from other family members such as grandparents. On the whole, this is to be avoided because it really doesn't help the sufferer – and it may add to their feelings that you are ashamed of them and what they are doing. It is generally better to be honest, although you may want to limit who knows.

Having a child who is self harming challenges a lot of the most basic instincts of parenting, and the strain can be immense. It raises all the usual emotional reactions, but also the question of why this has happened. Many parents admit that this soul-searching, and the blame other people often attach to parents, is the hardest part. Of course, one of the other difficulties parents face is that they want to know everything, do everything, support their child and, just as they have done through countless childhood illnesses, make everything better.

Why you may not be the best person to support your child

On finding out a child is self harming, most parents want to take control immediately, plan how to deal with this problem, and start working on sorting it out. It is incredibly difficult to accept that actually their child may be better able to talk to others outside of the family. In fact, it is often other people who find out first, and parents may be the last to know what has been going on. It is very common for parents to feel hurt, or even angry that they did not find out sooner, and this can make deciding what to do next even harder. Try not to take it too personally if your child has spoken to someone else instead of you. Most young people prefer talking to someone who is detached from the family about their self harm – or in fact about any emotional problems. It is often about them feeling safer, as they can say whatever they need to and not worry about the repercussions at home. It can also be about keeping control: if they talk to someone whom they only see once a week in one place, then they know that discussion of that issue will only happen then – when they expect it and can prepare for it. If they tell you – Mum or Dad – then the issue is suddenly always around, and they may worry that they would never know when you were thinking about it or wanting to talk about it. Just as you might prefer to talk to a counsellor or a stranger about something that was troubling you, rather than to someone you see every day, they might do the same.

Remember also how your child may worry about the impact what they are doing has on you. Self harm is something that people do when they are desperately trying to cope with what is going on around them. They may be trying to deal with things without having to worry you. Teenagers and young people often make bad judgements and end up in trickier situations than they started out in – and self harm is no different. It isn't easy to come to your parents and admit that things are not going according to plan. Children are very discerning about the effect of issues like self harm on their parents, and often seeing the pain their parents experience is too difficult for them to handle on top of their own feelings. This is not to say that parents must hide their feelings, but that they should try to understand why their child has sought help from outside the family. All you can do as a parent is try to let them know that they can come to you if they need support. Keep communication open and make sure they know that you love them.

About blame

This issue is one that nearly all parents struggle with. You may even find that you and your partner disagree about it, and it can lead to disagreements over what to do or not do. Remember, usually parents do not single-handedly cause their child to self harm. As mentioned throughout this book, self harm is something that people do to cope with a whole host of emotions, memories and feelings that are made worse by the way they think and how they handle those things. It is true that parents sometimes have made things worse or are part of the problem. Sometimes, though, it's as simple as parents just being human. No human is perfect, and as parents we make mistakes just as we do in the rest of our life. So don't be too hard on yourself. You did not deliberately set out to hurt your child, and chances are that if you had done things differently, this may well still have happened. Don't be too keen to take all the blame upon yourself. You may feel a lot of shame and may worry about what other people will think. Many parents, sadly, do experience bad reactions from friends, colleagues and so on once it comes out that their child is having problems. But anyone who knows anything about self harm will know that it is not all your fault. If their ignorance leads them to blame you, do not go along with that.

Do not go it alone

If you are a parent trying to care for a child who is self harming, you may feel very strongly that it isn't *you* who needs help but *them*! You may find it frustrating when people offer you help. But, at the risk of annoying you even more, it really is a good idea for you to have somewhere you can go to offload all that you are feeling and carrying around inside of you. It will help you and also make you more effective at caring for your child. Even professionals dealing with issues like this get support (referred to as supervision), and although in your case it may be less official (regular coffee with a friend often works well), it is just as important. Talking to someone who is not directly involved with the situation may give you a different perspective, allow you to share honestly instead of hiding and covering up your emotions, and also give you another source for ideas and suggestions.

If you find self harm is threatening your family, don't just sit and worry or feel guilty. Many people are too afraid to do anything for fear of making things worse. But the most important thing is that you do *something*. No matter how old your child seems on the outside, someone who is self harming is communicating that they need some help. So don't be afraid to take steps yourself to start looking for where best to find it.

13 Notes and special considerations for professionals

If your job or something you do as a volunteer brings you into regular contact with those at risk of self harm – that is, almost any job that involves spending time with young people, medical or caring roles and even positions in churches or community centres – you need to know that if you were to come across a case, you would know how to deal with it.

Being well prepared to support people who are self harming involves more than just a knowledge of the issues covered already in this book; it requires organizations to be operating good policies and procedures covering all the related issues. The idea of having these in place is to make sure that wherever there is the potential for tricky situations to arise, what you do and don't do in those circumstances has been thought out in advance. Sometimes doing 'the right thing' is hard and may even feel wrong. It is much easier to define what should happen in advance than to decide in the heat of the moment.

This chapter aims to present an overview of the issues involved in caring for those who are self harming. Please be aware that no brief discussion in a book like this can do all that needs to be done for any organization that is encountering self harm. It is essential that these topics are discussed at a leadership level. It is always better to think about such potentially difficult issues *before* they are encountered.

About boundaries in working with those who self harm
If you have ever worked to support someone who is fighting self harm – or indeed any emotional or psychological problem – you will have encountered the issue of boundaries, although you may not have used that word to describe it. 'Boundaries' are the imaginary lines between you and the people you are supporting, caring for, teaching or whatever your role involves. They are the lines that make it clear what kind of relationship you have with them: where it starts and where it stops; what is appropriate and what is not. A good boundary means that both people know what they can do and when they would be crossing that line. So teachers can have fun with the pupils they teach, but students need to know that ultimately their teacher is not one of them. Pupils need to know that, if it comes down to it, they must do what that person says and recognize their authority. People who are confident at setting those boundaries do not need to be over-authoritative, and they also have no problem in maintaining their position when they need to.

Keeping clear boundaries is important in any professional relationship, and there are many excellent books written on this subject.[6] Boundaries are particularly key in a supportive relationship, because the nature of that relationship is that it can become very important to the person seeking support. Boundaries protect both parties – the person being supported and you as the person caring for them. Good, clear boundaries help people feel safe and secure, and enable them to share, make changes and move on.

Some people who self harm find accepting appropriate boundaries very difficult. This may be because they have such a low opinion of themselves that they do not see why

---

6 One recommendation is the series of books by Henry Cloud and John Townsend, the main one being *Boundaries: When to Say Yes, How to Say No, to Take Control of Your Life* (Zondervan, 2002).

anybody would care for them. They find friendships and relationships incredibly hard because they feel so vulnerable, constantly expecting people to let them down or find out what they are 'really like'. They find it difficult to explain how they are feeling when things are hard, and they constantly fear being alone. These people sometimes find that self harm – because it is so powerful a communicator of how bad they are feeling – is a very successful way of triggering care. Some may find that the phase when people found out about their self harm was the first time that anyone had looked after them and cared for them. This quite natural stage can then lead to a situation in which they find it very difficult to move beyond a certain point in recovery, because they fear that without their 'problem' there would be no reason for people to care for them. This can lead them to start trying to test the boundaries of a relationship in order to see how much people care. Other sufferers may find boundaries challenging simply because they have never experienced them, or because their own boundaries have been so badly violated in the past – for example, if they have experienced abuse. Examples of behaviour that tests or pushes boundaries might include: someone contacting you at difficult times and threatening to harm if you are not able to visit or call them; someone testing you by, for instance, leaving a meeting and seeing whether you notice; or someone persistently contacting you at home or at inappropriate times.

The problem with boundaries is that once they have been broken down, they are difficult to reinstate. A very painful aspect of broken boundaries is the impact on both the sufferer and the carer. If a sufferer oversteps the boundaries of their relationship with the carer, the carer feels hunted down and threatened, often instinctively resenting having their compassion 'forced'. Many end up withdrawing from the relationship. Most sufferers, meanwhile, hate that they are behaving in such a manipulative way. Very few ever set out to do so, and for most it is part of the effect that their overwhelming emotions are having on their lives, making their behaviour erratic and chaotic. A lot of manipulative behaviour is fuelled by fear: fear of abandonment, fear of who they are, fear of what they are facing and fear that no one will understand it. The sad reality is that if these patterns develop, many will have those fears confirmed when the people caring for them run out of patience.

Some people naturally test boundaries straight away; for others it can start as a relationship develops. It is vital to be clear from the start – and to be aware of where boundaries lie before someone tries to overstep them. Some people (such as counsellors and those who meet up more formally) actually like to have a written contract that each person signs at the beginning of a therapeutic relationship. Other people (such as youth leaders and teachers) often operate to a written policy that sets out the rules and boundaries of what their support can and cannot involve. So, for example, it might set out the hours in which someone can be contacted, or make clear how contact can be initiated (by email not phone; by work phone not mobile). It is much better to make those things clear before you start, so that both parties are protected from the problems that can arise.

Let's look at one experience of boundaries being tested, from a youth worker who was supporting a young person who self harmed:

'She would often ring me and talk for hours about her desire to self harm. I would try to talk her out of it. Very rarely did this work. She would still harm, and I would be shattered from the late night conversations and demoralized that what I said didn't help. In the end I made a boundary that meant she was not to ring when she wanted to self harm. Instead, she could ring after she had harmed or the urge had passed, and discuss

*how she felt, what triggered it and where she could go
from here. This meant she was not punished, and was
still able to call, but I found my role was changed and
it made it clear that it wasn't my job to stop her from
harming.*

*'But then I started to find she would ring or text me
at all times. If I didn't respond because I was asleep, she
would panic and start ringing and texting incessantly
until she got an answer. When she couldn't get hold of
me she thought she wouldn't be able to cope and she
would panic. I had to make it really clear to her that not
being available in the middle of the night did not mean
I didn't care! I created another boundary that between
11 p.m. and 8 a.m. I wouldn't answer the phone, and
I explained that I needed time when I could rest and
switch off so I could be better able to support her during
the day. Tackling matters head on dissolved the issue,
and she stopped ringing outside the boundaries that
had been set. Then, when much later she did once call
after 11, I felt able to respond because I knew it must be
genuinely important – and it turned out she had harmed
very seriously and needed taking to hospital.'*

By the way, the boundaries set in this example are still very
broad, and many would be more restricting than this. But
setting these clear boundaries helped both people feel more
secure and strengthened the supportive relationship they
had.

Think about where *your* boundaries are. For example,
before you give out a telephone number, think about what
this means. Avoid using personal (home) numbers where
possible and either use a work one or a mobile that you
can switch off when you are not available. If you regularly
support people, then you might want to think about getting a
second mobile specifically for this purpose. Email is simpler

because of the nature of it, but still be aware of the need to set clear limits. For example, if you only pick up email once a day, make this clear. Otherwise someone might misinterpret your failure to respond as a rejection.

Confidentiality

Confidentiality is a very important issue. People seeking support or wishing to talk to you will understandably want reassurance that you will keep what they say confidential, and they need to feel safe in what they share with you. However, it is important that you never promise absolute confidentiality, in case something is shared that needs to be taken elsewhere as part of a child protection policy, or as a legal requirement (for example, if you were to become aware that someone was involved in committing certain criminal offences). The best approach is to reassure someone that what they tell you will never be shared inappropriately, and that you will always inform them if other people need to be involved. Remember to make clear that if you did ever have to talk to someone else, you would explain the reasons why to them first, and then only share relevant (necessary) information. That way they can feel in control of who knows what and need not fear that other people will be talking about them without their knowledge.

It is very important that organizations keep clear policies relating to confidentiality. You should know exactly when it is necessary for you to break confidentiality (for example, to discuss something with a superior, tell parents if a child or minor is involved, or report children or vulnerable adults who may be at risk). If your organization does not have such a policy, ask them why!

Do be careful about confidentiality. It is such a vital part of caring for people, but one that is so often broken accidentally. Watch out for quick chats about people in the corridor (you never know who is round the corner and might hear), offices that are not soundproofed and documents on computer screens that are left on. Be particularly careful about emails, which are not a secure form of communication and can go astray, and watch what you leave as a message on answering machines – it may be that the person who picks up the message is not the one you left it for.

Child/vulnerable adult protection

At times, as part of supporting those who are self harming, you may have disclosed to you information that brings to your attention the fact that a child or vulnerable adult may be at risk of serious harm – either because of their self harm or from another person. It is very important that you take this seriously and that you make the right decisions about what you do with that information.

All organizations working with people who are potentially at risk from any source (be aware that this includes not just children but all young people and vulnerable adults, such as those who are struggling with any emotional, psychological or psychiatric disorder) should have an up-to-date child protection policy. Make sure you know what it says. It is too late if you look it up after the situation has already arisen. Be prepared!

If your concern relates to the self harm that person is experiencing, then it can be difficult to ascertain whether they are at serious risk or not. Some people self harm for many years at what might be called a 'low level' and never experience significant (that is, life-threatening) harm. Others very quickly move on to struggle with suicidal feelings or serious harm. Organizations that encounter self harm regularly might want to draw up a formal policy stating the point at which action should be taken and the time when someone is considered at potential risk. This is much better than trying to decide it on a case-by-case basis. As a guide, here are some of the conditions we feel would be an indicator that someone might be at more serious risk. If any of these are present, we would advise taking further action (for example, seeking medical advice and contacting parents/guardians/social services) straight away to keep that person safe. Remember, making a judgement call in these cases is not easy even for professionals, so don't try to do it yourself if you are not qualified.

* If there have been previous episodes of self harm that have required hospital or medical treatment.

* If self harm episodes are, or ever have been, linked with alcohol or drug intoxication, or if that person also struggles with a drug or alcohol problem.

* If there is a risk of death from their form of self harm (for example, if they are overdosing) or if there is any evidence of suicidal thoughts or intent.

* If self harm ever occurs when they are not consciously aware of what they are doing – that is, they are dissociating (see Chapter 4, page 39) or are under the influence of drugs or alcohol.

* If anyone else is at risk because of their self harm (such as younger children or dependent vulnerable adults).

Please remember that there are no hard and fast rules where self harm is concerned. Do keep an eye out for when self harm seems to be escalating or where someone is very emotionally distressed. Support from you – no matter how good – is never a substitute for them seeking appropriate medical care. Whatever someone's situation they should always be in touch with their GP.

Suicidal thoughts and suicide attempts

As already discussed, suicidal feelings and the feelings that surround self harm are often closely related. It is vital that people working with self harmers are aware that sufferers may start to struggle with suicidal thoughts. Suicide is not a dirty word, and it is much better to talk about it and be open about it. Do not be afraid to ask someone you are supporting whether they have ever felt suicidal. You will not 'put ideas into their heads' or make them more likely to attempt suicide. In fact, it is much more likely that by bringing those feelings out into the open you will be able to help them to get the help they need.

Professional guidelines recommend that anyone who has ever seriously self harmed (for example, to the point of needing medical treatment) should be assessed by a mental health professional. (This is likely to be a child/adolescent psychiatrist or a specialist mental health worker, though some GPs may be happy to assess and oversee minor cases.) One thing that should be checked in that assessment is the suicide risk. This is very important because the suicide risk is so much higher in people who are self harming. Make sure it happens!

Meanwhile, if someone does disclose to you their plan to attempt suicide, be aware of where you stand legally. To aid or be involved with a suicide is illegal. This means that if someone tells you they plan to take their life, giving details that would enable you to intervene and stop them, and you do not, you could be breaking the law. Remember, somebody needs to intervene – though it may be that it is more appropriate for someone else to respond rather than you. The police or local social services can do so, with paramedics if needed. If you are able to deal with it yourself, always try to have someone else with you (another member of your team if you are working for an organization, or a friend if you are a carer), and always seek additional help afterwards, even if you are able to make sure that they are no longer in any physical risk. Your local A&E will be able to advise and make a referral to the local mental health team, as will your GP or out of hours service.

Much more common than clear suicide plans are the kinds of situation in which someone has made a vague comment about wanting to 'end it all', or in which a teenager has told their friends that they are thinking of suicide. This may be done in a manipulative way (threatening suicide if people don't respond). The golden rule here is to always take people seriously if they share that they are thinking of trying to commit suicide. The urban myth that if they talk about it they will not do it simply *is not true*. Most studies show that people who attempt suicide have usually mentioned it to someone in the days or weeks beforehand. Even if the person you are caring for is talking about suicide in a manipulative way, it's important to remember that many young people who attempt suicide do view it as a 'tool' they can use to try to change situations. Teenagers and young people often think and talk about suicide in an irrational way, as if they would get to take part in and benefit from the long-term outcomes related to their own suicide. Making judgements about who might or might not attempt suicide is very difficult, so don't try to do it if you are not qualified – always get the professionals involved and keep that person safe. This is particularly the case with teenagers: studies show that many who attempt suicide consider it for a very short time beforehand and may do so extremely impulsively. There may not be much warning or chance to intervene. So if you are aware that someone is having spells of feeling suicidal, take action and get them some support.

Thinking about the issues involved in suicidal feelings can be very depressing and can make carers feel helpless. But remember: it isn't true that if someone wants to end their life there is nothing anyone can do. Actually, good care and someone who is able to sit and talk to them about how they are feeling often can make a difference. So, the most important thing for you to do as a carer or as someone supporting them is to help that person access better support. You may not be able to prevent someone's suicide at the end of the day; but never leave yourself in a position of wondering whether you should have taken action. If in doubt, act.

About children and their parents/guardians
Self harm as a phenomenon is developing and spreading in the UK. As it does so, the age range of those suffering also seems to be broadening. On average, self harm starts at age twelve or older, but it is not unusual now to see younger children starting to self harm. This means that for every younger sufferer you are supporting there are also parents and a worried family somewhere behind the scenes.

If you work for an organization, it should have clear guidelines on when steps should be taken to inform parents/ guardians of concerns about their child. Some organizations may wish to inform parents if they become aware that *any* self harm is occurring, whereas others (generally those working with older teenagers) may only do so if the young person may be at risk or is refusing to see their GP. Please make sure you are aware of the policy your organization works under, and, if they do not have one, suggest that one is drawn up!

On the whole, teenagers in the UK aged sixteen and above are given the same right to consent to their own treatment as adults are. That means they can seek treatment on their own and their parents do not need to be informed or to consent on their behalf. Even under-sixteens can be given this right if they are judged to be able to assess the decision and all the possible relevant factors in an adult way (this is known as proving 'Gillick competence'). However, decisions regarding those who are under sixteen are always tricky, and in such a potentially serious situation, they should always be overseen by a doctor or other health care professional.

Real-life experiences...
Where are you now?

NINA

*'I'm at a place where I sometimes think how weird this is!
I work in a job with a lot of responsibility and hold a lot of
things together, looking as if I'm the most normal, stable person
in the world. Then sometimes it's like I can't cope any more,
and cutting or burning seems like a sensible way to deal with it.
Fortunately, these days I can usually see that it's actually a very
bad way to cope with it before I actually do it. I only slipped up
three times last year, which from daily making my arm bleed by
picking existing cuts, if not making new ones, is actually quite
a lot of progress, even though it's not the complete recovery I'm
moving towards.*

*'The path towards recovery and taking steps on it has been
so hard. I've realized that I can't get better by myself, and that
means admitting to people what I've done and that I'm not
as perfect as I look on the outside. Fortunately, I was already
having some counselling when I first struggled with this, and
managing to be honest with my counsellor was probably what
stopped things getting completely out of control because there
was a degree of accountability. I think if I'd had to deal with
it completely by myself it would have got far, far worse. She
directed me towards a website where, to start with, I could reach
out for help anonymously. I registered, and by using the forums
I can post anything about how I feel and know no one is going
to put me in the loony bin and no one is going to know it's me
who said it – I use a false name!*

*'While that was helpful, I've also needed a real person
to talk to sometimes – someone who knows me well and who
connects a bit with my day-to-day life. And I found it was
nightmarishly hard being vulnerable. I started with someone*

I knew I wouldn't see again for at least a year but who I could text if I needed her to pray, and then I told another friend I don't see a lot of but who I talk to on the phone quite regularly. I felt as if it would be less of a burden to them because I don't see them day to day so they'd not feel as if they had to be looking out for me all the time. Then, finally I told two people close by who I see on a regular basis. Initially, telling people made me feel worse and such a failure that it almost made me want to harm more! I also found that it was hard to tell them in advance when I was tempted to do it... I hesitate in case I'm manipulating people or in case I'm using harming as my way of telling someone I'm hurting rather than learning to verbalize what the problem is. I was also worried that I might be attention-seeking. So I'd often end up telling them afterwards when it was too late for them to help. What I did find then, though, was that they could encourage me not to panic about what I'd done, to let it heal rather than make it worse. And I found that being able to talk to someone made me feel as if it had less of a hold over me. It released me from that secretive cocoon, and I could get on with life again a bit quicker.

'These days I'm a bit better at seeing what makes me vulnerable. Around Christmas, around my birthday, going to weddings and if I'm physically ill for any length of time and it's wearing me down – those are the times when it begins to feel that everything is too much to deal with. There are often other things going on too – being busy at work or letting my diary get too full. I'm learning that at those times I need to put something into operation before I get to the stage where I want to hurt myself. I'm learning to try to verbalize how I'm feeling to "safe" people, that it's ok to express negative emotion or to be upset, and that it's ok to share that with other people.

'When I feel like someone understands my hurt or the way I feel or is sharing the pain with me, it makes me far less likely to do myself harm because I don't feel so alone in it. I have a real sense that this is not how I want to live, and these days when I am tempted I try very hard not to give in. Occasionally I fail. Then I try to tell someone because I find it has less power over me if I do so. I also know they will ask if I've done it again, so then there is a degree of accountability while I'm still vulnerable. It's been a hard ride and it still is sometimes, but I'm changing and I hope I'm well on the way to recovery and to being able to reach out and help others. I understand what it's like to hurt and not be able to express it in a good way. I'd love to be able to provide a safe environment for other people to share how they're feeling so that they can begin to find a degree of healing in doing so.'

JIM

'After starting counselling I did everything I could to free myself from the addiction and the darkness. Then I had to write an essay in an exam about what God was doing in my life, and I started writing about my self harm. As I put the pen down I just felt free. To this day I have never cut myself on purpose again.

'The darkness still comes to me, but the controlling-ness of it all just went. When a number of months had gone by and I was still able to not cut myself I knew it was a fresh start. I still struggled sometimes with thoughts about wanting to die, but I wanted to want to live! It took time but I have just started to experience what it feels like to actually want to live. What a journey!'

RACHAEL

'The road to recovery from self harm and depression has been a long one. It has taken me about three or four years so far. I gradually got to the place where I could stop myself from self harming. I discussed this with my psychologist, and we agreed that I no longer needed a contract.

'Often I take ten steps forward and five steps back. So I might stop self harming for say three to six months at a time, but then I have one slip-up and it takes a while to break the cycle again. I have found that once I start self harming again after a long period of not self harming I seem to do it again and again, but I am finding myself able to break the cycle quicker and quicker every time. Recovery is up and down. There will be times when you soar and times when you crawl, times when you are doing well and times when you feel you go back to old ways of coping.

'I'm not sure if I will ever say I am going to be self harm free forever. I think I will always have a weakness and a tendency to turn to self harm as a coping strategy. About six months ago I had been self harm free for quite a long period of time and I thought I would never do it again, but when my mood dipped and circumstances meant I was in a depressed state again, I did turn to self harm once more.

'Writing this now I have been self harm free for the last three or four months, and I am in a place of being very content and happy with life. I don't know what the future has in store for me but I have a feeling that now I have more tools to be able to cope with whatever might come my way.'

LIBBY

'Right now I am at a point when it is coming up to two years since I harmed. Although I still don't fully understand how to cope in certain situations and how to react, it's good to know I don't need to harm to get some sort of feeling.

'In a crisis I do always think about doing it again but I know I don't need it, which calms me a little. I stress out and over-think everything and start to panic. I'm very paranoid about everything; when I do stress I can't think rationally about the situation and always go to extremes about things. I think this is because of the self harm, and using that as an escape from the problem.

'I stopped self harming using a combination of will power and help from other people. When I had bad days during that time it *was the hardest thing to not cut; I felt like I was going to explode and got very angry about it all. A lot of the time, getting away from whatever was making me angry helped. I think everyone around me felt helpless because I didn't know what I needed but I know I needed to do it on my own.'*

Appendix: Minimizing and disguising scars

Scar reduction

In order to approach methods of scar reduction properly you need to understand what scarring is and the cycle of healing a wound goes through. When the body is wounded, it replaces injured areas with stronger, healthy tissue, in the hope that this stronger tissue will prevent further damage. This skin will usually have a different texture and tone – for example, it doesn't have the pigmentation to be able to tan, so if you do get a tan you'll notice it is patchy where you have scars. When a wound first begins to heal, the blood forms a latticed barrier to stop further bleeding. This then starts to form a scab. Behind the scab the skin starts to heal in from the edges until a new layer of skin has grown over and the scab will fall away. The new skin at this point will look red or pink in colour and will have a slightly 'fragile' appearance. This is the body's quick response to healing the wound, and it will take about a year for the skin to fade naturally to a more subtle tone. This is usually still lighter than the skin's natural tone, but you'll be surprised how well scars will blend in after a few years.

In some cases this process does not occur entirely according to plan, and instead of these subtle scars, what are called 'keloid' or 'hypertrophic' scars can develop. These are scars that are more noticeable, either in colour or texture. They can be angry red in colour or have more obvious peaks, troughs or bumps in the new skin that forms. This is not due to anything done to the wound, but to the way the individual's body deals with the healing process. A tendency to scar in this way may be genetic, and these types of scars tend to be associated with specific ethnic groups. You can't do much about it if you tend to scar in this way, but do be aware that your scars will be more obvious – it makes it doubly important that you take care of wounds.

In some cases plastic surgery may be an option to improve the appearance of scars, but even this leaves a mark, so it is not a perfect solution. It is important to do whatever you can to reduce the long-term damage.

INITIAL HEALING

The first step in scar reduction is to do everything you can to aid the healing process and maximize the chances of a wound healing with a small or faint scar. It is much better to avoid scars forming in the first place. The sooner after a harming episode that good first aid principles are used to care for the wounds, the quicker the body can begin to heal well. Many people who self harm can end up with scars being worsened because they don't treat their wounds initially. Simple things such as cleaning a wound will reduce infection and speed healing.

For cuts, what is most important is to ensure that the flesh is held together properly. If the cut is treated in hospital it is likely that this would be with stitches or with the surgical glue commonly administered in A&E departments. Stitches need to be applied in the first twenty-four hours after the cut has been made; after this the edges of the cut will have started to heal and will no longer fuse together to heal well with stitches. Surgical glue is very effective when used, as it does not leave the possibility of scarring where the stitches were. Glue acts by holding the wound together and then dissolving away as the wound heals. If you've ever used super glue and got your fingers stuck together you'll understand the principle. In the short term people sometimes feel a lump in the wound, but this is just the glue continuing to dissolve.

So how do you know whether a wound needs to be treated in hospital? How do you know whether it needs stitches to avoid scarring? Remember that there is no substitute for medical advice. If you are in any doubt, get some – from your GP surgery or from A&E. Alternatively, you can phone NHS Direct (UK only) for advice.[7] Their guidelines state that you need to seek advice if any of the following apply:

* There is significant blood loss; a wound won't hold closed due to its location and keeps opening up again; or a wound won't stop bleeding after ten minutes of applying pressure to it with a clean dressing.

* A wound is deeper than just a surface cut, so might involve tendons or more significant blood vessels.

* The wound involves the mouth, face, hand or genitals.[8]

If you decide to treat your wound yourself, home treatment is most effective through the use of steri-strips (available from most good chemists). These can be a bit pricey and fiddly to use, but they are well worth it for the results. To use, make sure the wound is clean and that the edges are dry – without this the strips will not hold to the skin and will be rendered useless. Stick one end of the strip to one side of the cut, and then, holding the wound shut, stick the other end of the strip firmly on the other side to close up the cut. Start by putting a steri-strip across the middle of the wound to align it properly, then work from the edge of the wound towards the middle, putting strips alternately on each edge. When completed, put a strip on each side of the wound, running perpendicular to the other strips to hold them down. Do this on both sides of the cut. If it looks as if it may pull open, then you can put more strips over the top of this. After this, cover

---

7 The number for NHS direct is 0845 4647.

8 Taken from 'Does my cut need stitches?', http://www.nhsdirect.nhs.uk/ articles/article.aspx?articleId=1048 (accessed Feb 08).

the wound and try to leave it alone to heal. After a couple of days, or if the dressing gets very messy, clean and re-dress the wound, keeping an eye out for any signs of infection (such as swelling, redness or pus).

When it comes to burns, the first thing to do is run the affected area under cool or tepid water, to cool it and stop tissue damage from progressing. This needs to be done within about twenty minutes of the burn occurring, and you need to persist with it for about ten to thirty minutes. Never pop any blisters yourself – they are the body's protective cushioning. Do not apply any creams, but do cover the burn with a sterile dressing. If it is painful, you can take a dose of a painkiller such as paracetamol or ibuprofen. But if the pain is very bad or you think the burn is getting worse, seek medical help as soon as possible. It's always important to cover a burn, so if you don't have a sterile dressing, use some cling film, or, if the burn is on your hand, a plastic bag. Then go straight to the doctor or to A&E. Note that for very large or deep burns you should always seek medical advice, as for any that are on the joints, face or hands.

Treatments to cover up scars

If you have ended up with scarring as a result of self harm, then it is worth trying out some of the various options for covering up or reducing that scarring. There are many specific treatments for scars. Remember, though, that none are quick fixes, and whatever you do is highly unlikely to lead to the scar becoming invisible. The most effective principles of scar reduction are about enabling the body to have the best facilities for healing, so you also need to be eating well and be in reasonable physical health. Otherwise nothing you rub into the skin is going to make any difference!

Make-up is one of the most laborious ways of concealing scars. This is not a solution for everyday use, but perhaps (if desperate) for a one-off special event or occasion. Colour matching to the skin is very difficult – believe it or not, it is actually more complicated to do so on your body than on your face! There are specialist producers of high-density products that are designed to give the best possible coverage, which are marketed to those with port wine birthmarks and facial scarring (ask your GP for more details). Meanwhile, if you have scarring with a pinkish colouring, most chemists stock green make-up that can be used to neutralize the colours. In all cases, of course, you have to get the application right in order not to draw more attention to the area, so look into getting someone to show you how to apply it correctly.

Silicone sheets are used like a pressure dressing, sealing in the scar and holding it down. They are now marketed fairly widely as an aid to healing and as something that can improve the appearance of scars – old and new. However, obviously they will have the most impact on more recent scars – within the first year of healing. They are often used on hypertrophic or keloid scars, as they are documented to have most success on raised scars or those that are particularly angry in colour. Silicone sheets come in dressing form with a gel side (which is the silicone) that sits against the wound. People who have used them find them quite soothing – especially if the wound is very itchy – as they keep the wound moist. Silicone sheets are now available from most chemists.

There are hundreds of **oils and creams** available on the high street that make claims about reducing scarring, from fade-out creams containing a small amount of steroid to intensive cocoa butter for scars and stretch marks and specialist Bio-Oil®. Always be sure to purchase any product from a reputable retailer, as some back street retailers sell creams that use combinations of chemicals that are unsafe and illegal to sell in this country. For any of these creams the thing to remember is that they need to be used day and night for a minimum of three months, if not six, before results start to show. So you need to be committed! Make sure you get medical advice before using any steroid-based cream, as they can thin and weaken the skin and should never be used on the face, genitals or on broken or still healing skin. Creams such as cocoa butter and Bio-Oil® are far less risky and don't need to cost the earth. They moisturize the skin and keep it smooth. Whether they are more effective than normal body moisturizer is unknown, but it supports the concept of indulging your skin to give it the best support to combat the scars, so you might feel it is worth a try!

Aloe vera gel is something people often find very soothing, and is also said to aid healing. It is available from most health food stores. After-sun cream often has aloe vera in it, and it really seems to cool the skin and soothe the sunburn (remember, you shouldn't use any creams on other kinds of burn whilst they are still healing). This is a product that, used immediately after the skin has healed over, would help and soothe. Longer-term impact on scars is unknown.

Vitamin E oil is another treatment people use, and many report good results. It doesn't offer miracle results but consistently improves the skin tone and leaves it really nourished. Several high street stores have their own vitamin E ranges, all of which will have their benefits. Particularly recommended is the use of pure vitamin E oil. If it is for specific use on scars only, vitamin E capsules (the ones you'd normally swallow) are a good way to get the oil in a single dose, and they are usually highly concentrated and thicker, making it easier to apply. They are also a lot cheaper than buying skin treatments. Just break the capsule open and rub in the oil.

Some self-harm websites recommend **tattoos**, the idea being that when a scar fades to lighter than the skin tone, it can then be tattooed to match the original skin tone. The principle sounds fine, but tattooing scar tissue is very different from tattooing normal skin, and it varies from person to person. Often the skin will not hold the ink evenly, giving a patchy effect that can stand out more than the scar did before. Also, this only works if you do not tan, because the scar will again be lighter than the rest of the skin, and tattoos can fade when exposed to the sun. This one is to be used with caution!

Finally, **surgery** is an option that many look into but few actually go through with, as it is expensive and, depending on which type is used, unreliable. The aim of conventional surgery is to take scars that have healed badly and remove the scar tissue, re-sealing the skin in a manner that will give less scarring; in some cases the scar tissue is burnt off. This can understandably be very uncomfortable. In some rare cases NHS doctors will make referrals for this type of work, but the recipient will have to be able to prove they have not self harmed for a minimum of two years; however, most work is done privately. **Laser surgery** burns away tissue in the area that is scarred in a very similar way to tattoo removal. This involves multiple appointments and can be very painful, sometimes leaving the patient with a burn-like sensation. This can work very well, but it can also leave the person with a scar that is even worse. If you are considering any form of invasive or medical treatment for scarring always see your GP first and make sure you get referred to a reputable and experienced specialist.

Further support

For further help and support there are a variety of organizations and websites for those who are struggling with self harm.

Selfharm.co.uk is a new and growing charity offering information, resources, training and support to young people who self harm and to those around them, be they family members, friends or professionals. Amongst a range of exciting forthcoming projects they have plans to develop an innovative online therapeutic programme for young people. When this project has been established it is expected that it will be one of the largest national resources specifically designed to support young people who self harm.

Adullam Ministries is a Christian organization providing support to those who self harm. Their website offers forums as well as links to more information and training courses for carers and others who are involved with self harmers (http://adullam-ministries.org.uk).

Young people and self harm is a website run by the National Children's Bureau (http://www.selfharm.org.uk/default.aspa). This is a very informative website with good links to local support available in some areas, although it is not being updated any more.

The website **http://www.selfharmuk.org** contains the results of a national enquiry into self harm in young people which was run by Camelot in conjunction with the Mental Health Foundation. The report, 'Truth Hurts', was published in 2006 and can be downloaded from the site. This site is good for professionals and those interested in finding out more, but is not really aimed at sufferers themselves.

Lifesigns (http://www.lifesigns.org.uk) is a UK-run, web-based organization run by people with personal experience of self harm. It includes mailing lists, message boards and all kinds of other information for sufferers.

Saneline is an organization offering support to anyone struggling with mental illness. Their website offers some information about self harm (http://www.sane.org.uk/ AboutMentalIllness/Self-harm), and they also run an evening telephone helpline for anyone struggling with how they are feeling (0845 767 8000, 6 p.m. to 11 p.m.).

For help and advice, particularly 24-hour telephone helplines:

NHS Direct is a 24-hour source of health information and advice. Call them on 0845 4647 or visit their website (http://www.nhsdirect.nhs.uk).

The Samaritans also run a 24-hour helpline for anyone struggling with how they are feeling. Call them on 08457 90 90 90, email on jo@samaritans.org or write to Chris at P.O. Box 9090, Stirling FK8 2SA.